D1251433

The Behavior of Interest Rates

THE
BEHAVIOR
OF
INTEREST
RATES An Application
of the Efficient Market Model
to U.S. Treasury Bills

RICHARD ROLL

Foreword by Paul Samuelson

BASIC BOOKS, INC., PUBLISHERS

New York, London

332.8
R 74b
Copy 2

© 1970 by Basic Books, Inc.
Library of Congress Catalog Card Number: 76-126951
SBN 465-00597-7
Manufactured in the United States of America

To A. G. R., *amante*

MAY 17 '72

HUNT LIBRARY
CARNEGIE-MELLON UNIVERSITY

Introduction to the

Irving Fisher Award Series

This volume is the first in a projected series of Irving Fisher Award Monographs, sponsored by Omicron Delta Epsilon, the International Honor Society in Economics. The author of the volume, Professor Richard Roll of Carnegie-Mellon University, is the winner of the first annual competition for monographs by graduate students or recent Ph.Ds. Each entry was first judged by a Selection Committee in the entrant's own department, with the winner moving to one of nine Regional Selection Boards. The regional winners were entered in the finals and judged by a board composed of Professors Kenneth J. Arrow, Kenneth E. Boulding, Milton Friedman, Paul A. Samuelson, and Egon Neuberger (*ex officio*). I wish to take this opportunity to thank the members of the Departmental Selection Committees and Regional Selection Boards, and Professors Arrow, Boulding, Friedman, and Samuelson. Without the generous support of these eminent economists, the series would not have been possible.

The idea that competitions open to students and junior members of our profession would provide a useful forum and creative challenge to these future leaders of the profession originated with the members of the Executive Board of Omicron Delta Epsilon. They felt that the Honor Society could perform a service by sponsoring these competitions. With the wholehearted support of the members of the Executive Board and Board of Trustees, and particularly Professors Ervin K. Zingler, President of ODE, and Alan A. Brown, Chairman of the Board of Trustees of ODE, this idea has now been brought to fruition. I wish to thank Dr. Geza Feketekuty, who, as associate editor, helped me in initiating the series, and Professor Richard Dusansky, who took over this position and is working with me to improve the competitions. Basic Books, Inc. and their Senior Editor, Martin Kessler, had the vision to agree to support the Irving Fisher Award and to publish the winning entries before it was clear that the series would prove to be a successful venture. I applaud their entrepreneurial spirit.

In the final analysis, it is the quality of the entries that determines the success of any competition. I am grateful to those who entered the competitions and hope that in future years we shall have an even greater number of outstanding entries. This, plus the dedicated work of the leaders of our profession willing to serve as judges, can make the Irving Fisher Award Series an important asset to the economics profession.

Now that I have introduced you to the Irving Fisher Award Series, I am happy to yield the floor to Professor Paul A. Samuelson, who has kindly agreed to introduce you to this volume, the first volume of the Irving Fisher Award.

Egon Neuberger
Editor
Irving Fisher Award Series

Foreword

PAUL A. SAMUELSON

Scientific research should be devoted to important questions. Here is one important question: Do organized speculative markets perform a socially useful function? There are two *standard* answers offered to this question: (1) A speculator is a fat man with a penchant for arithmetic who garners gobs of money for no good reason. (2) A speculator is a noble soul who takes risk upon his own shoulders so that producers of a chancy commodity can slough off risk by hedging operations and thereby reduce the cost to the consumer of goods that are subject to unpredictable acts of God, the weatherman, and the king's enemies.

These, I have been careful to say, are standard and hence rather superficial reactions. But they are replicated at a deeper scientific level of discourse. Maynard Keynes was a scientific genius. He was also a highly successful speculator. Therefore when he speaks on the subject of what organized bourses accomplish, his is a voice worth listening to. Keynes left us many memorable passages of prose: "In the long run we are all dead." Or the cadenza ending his classic *General Theory:* "the ideas of economists and political philosophers, both when they are right and when they are wrong are more powerful . . . ." And, among connoisseurs, there is the pre-Galbraithian prophecy of Keynes (in 1930) of affluence ahead and the problem of leisure that this would bring for humans, whose bodies and temperaments have developed through eons of evolution, equipped to earn their daily bread. His concern that release from the struggle for existence might result in a "nervous breakdown" perhaps provides insight into the quandary of affluent youth on our college campuses.

But among his *bons mots* are the following passages, highly relevant to appraisal of speculative markets:

> the energies and skill of the professional investor and speculator are mainly occupied . . . , not with making superior long-term forecasts of the probable yield of an investment over its whole life, but with foreseeing changes in the conventional basis of valuation a short time ahead of the general public . . . . The social object of skilled investment should be to defeat the dark forces of time and ignorance which envelop our future. The actual, private object of the most skilled investment to-day is "to beat the gun," as the Americans so well express it, to outwit the crowd, and to pass the bad, or depreciating, half-crown to the other fellow . . . it is, so to speak, a game of Snap, of Old Maid, of Musical Chairs—a pastime in which he is victor who says *Snap* neither too soon nor too late, who passes the Old Maid to his neighbour before the game is over, who secures a chair for himself when the music stops . . . . Or, to change the metaphor slightly, professional investment may be likened to those newspaper competitions in which the competitors have to pick out the six prettiest faces from a hundred photographs, the prize being awarded to the competitor whose choice most nearly corresponds to the average preferences of the competitors as a whole; so that each competitor has to pick, not those faces which he himself finds prettiest, but those which he thinks likeliest to catch the fancy of the other competitors . . . .[1]

Since Keynes was a notoriously successful investor, this adverse judgment on competitive markets is deemed worthy of special weight. And yet, a lifetime of scientific research by Holbrook Working at Stanford's Research Institute led him to the finding that prices quoted on the Board of Trade produced that pattern of carry-over from years of dearth to years of plenty which a technocrat would prescribe as optimal. This is a far cry from the Keynes witticism: "It is said, for example, that the shares of American companies which manufacture ice tend to sell at a higher price in summer when their profits are seasonally high than in winter when no one wants ice."[2]

And so we have, at a more sophisticated level, a reprise of the polar contentions that the ticker tape reveals God's wisdom, or that it spins a tale, told by an idiot, full of sound and fury, signifying nothing. The present book by Richard Roll offers a significant contribution to this important debate. Roll measures the facts against plausible theoretical models. I shall not presume to interpret his findings. That is a privilege reserved for the reader. But I hope it will be in order to call attention to Roll's grappling with a fascinating problem that once challenged my own research efforts. "How can the market price of a stock—say General Motors—ever be other than 'correct'? For if it were quoted at *patently* bargain levels, sharpeyed speculators would already have turned to it and bid up its price." This bit of wisdom undulates tantalizingly between irrefutable (and hence uninteresting) truism and gratuitous assertion. My own offering in the matter was to prove the deductive theorem: For very general stochastic processes, the changes in the expected value of a future variable, as new random data become available, cancel out to zero, or to a systematic bias inherent in investor risk aversion. Dr. Roll has, happily, gone beyond deduction to hypothesis formation and verification and I commend his vintage.

NOTES

1. John Maynard Keynes, *General Theory of Employment, Interest, and Money* (New York: Harcourt, Brace and World, 1936), pp. 154-156.
2. *Ibid.*, p. 154.

Acknowledgments

Professor Eugene Fama guided this research from inception to conclusion. Professors Reuben Kessel and Arnold Zellner also spent much time providing valuable criticisms and suggestions.

The informal workshop organized by finance students at the University of Chicago was an invaluable sounding board and an avid critic. Its members who aided this research are Marshall Blume, Philip Brown, David Duvel, Michael C. Jensen, and Myron Scholes.

Professors Merton Miller and Roger Waud also provided many useful comments and suggestions.

The Chicago office of Merrill Lynch, Pierce, Fenner and Smith, government securities division, provided access to files containing the price quotations that constitute the data sample.

Contents

Figures

Tables

The Behavior of Interest Rates

Chapter 1

Introduction

PRICE BEHAVIOR IN COMPETITIVE MARKETS

A favorite academic model of security price behavior in competitive markets is the multiplicative random walk

$$P_{j,t} = P_{j,t-1} \exp(U_{j,t} + R_{j,t}) \qquad (1\text{-}1)$$

where $P_{j,t}$ is the price[1] of security j at time t, $R_{j,t}$ is some "normal" or "competitive" rate of return appropriate for security j, and $U_{j,t}$ is a random variable, independently and identically distributed over time. If security j follows the process described by equation 1-1 and if $R_{j,t} = R_j$, a constant for all time, then the price change, as measured by the log price relative, $\log_e(P_{j,t}/P_{j,t-1})$, will be serially independent. This follows from the independence assumption about $U_{j,t}$ by a simple rearrangement of (1-1).

This model is interesting for two reasons. *First*, it is supposed to make sense theoretically: When a market is competitive in the classic sense, every trader has perfect information and serial dependence in price changes is immediately discovered. Serial dependence in price changes implies that *costless* mechanical trading rules earn posi-

3

tive profits but economic profit cannot persist in a competitive market. If such profits should arise, they will
soon be erased, along with their cause (the serial dependence), by competition. A *second* reason for the model's
popularity is its ability to describe empirical data well. This
has been demonstrated, for example, by Fama, who shows
that some common stock log price relatives are indeed
serially uncorrelated (1965, p. 72, Table 10).

Despite its empirical success, the random walk model
has been partly discredited on a theoretical basis by
Mandelbrot (1966), who has pointed out that mechanical trading rules will not be profitable even if market
price only follows a submartingale sequence.[2] A submartingale sequence is a weaker condition than a random
walk,[3] and competition will probably not cause a stronger
condition to prevail when a weaker condition is sufficient.

Mandelbrot's suppositions will be used here in presenting
and testing a model of securities markets, the "efficient
market model," whose name comes from its assumption
that competitive securities markets efficiently incorporate
new information into price (i.e., they incorporate information very rapidly and without error).

PURPOSES OF THIS INVESTIGATION

Briefly outlined, the purposes of this investigation are
(1) to present a formal statement of the efficient market
model of security price behavior; (2) to use theories of
the term structure of interest rates and the efficient market model to derive exact representations of the dynamic
behavior of internal rates of return (which are simple
transforms of prices) for noncoupon, fixed-maturity bonds;

(3) to present empirical evidence of the actual dynamic behavior of internal rates of return for U.S. Treasury bills; (4) to test different term structure hypotheses; and (5) to test the efficiency, in terms of the model, of the U.S. Treasury bill market.

NOTES

1. Including dividend or interest accrual from period $t-1$.
2. A submartingale sequence is defined algebraically by equation (2-4).
3. In fact, a random walk is a special case of a submartingale.

Chapter 2

The Efficient Market Model

ON THE MEANING OF PROFITABLE SECURITY TRADING SYSTEMS

In competitive equilibrium, the entrepreneur endowed with no specialized skill receives no excess income over existing alternative employments. This venerable economic doctrine naturally applies to an investor engaged in the occupation of trading securities and to his information-processing equipment. Intelligent people can expect to earn a satisfactory income by trading securities, but equal success is likely to follow the same time spent in other occupations.

It is difficult, if not impossible, to determine whether security traders are receiving rent. One must first be able to distinguish between expected and ex post rent. Only the former will attract new entrants into the industry and only the latter is observable. Purely random fluctuations in security prices make some traders wealthy regardless of their skill. In this sense, they have earned rent ex post, but their gains may be offset by the negative economic profits of others so that no rent is earned in the aggregate. Second, how is one to distinguish between the random success just described and success due to nonspecific skill? Since skill is distributed unevenly, it must be partly responsible for the differing incomes of security traders. Finally, there may be some individuals who *do* possess specialized skills and resources. Among these might be talkative corporate insiders who are friends, but it is difficult to think of other examples, and few economists would even list clairvoyance as a specialized skill since it is equally valued in other activities.

We are uncertain what part each of the three factors, luck, skill, and specific resources, plays in a given financial success. It therefore seems unlikely that a direct measurement of profit will provide a meaningful yardstick to gauge the competitiveness of a securities market. Fortunately, we may pass to indirect measurement and ask how observed market phenomena, particularly prices, should behave under competitive conditions. If actual prices do behave in the predicted way, we are entitled to conclude that the market is competitive.

TEMPORAL PRICE BEHAVIOR

How will security prices behave over time under competitive trading conditions? A direct application of marginal productivity theory can provide an answer. Here, the product is information, and, more specifically, it is probability distributions on the future values of securities. The productive resources include the investor's natural perspicacity, his educational training in data analysis and institutional facts, communication and computation equipment, and time spent in analyzing data, visiting executives, and reading financial news. At the margin, the con-

tribution of each of these resources to the investor's per-
ceived knowledge of the security should bear a constant
proportion to its per unit resource cost.

We immediately ascertain that low-cost resources will
have been well tested by competitors and are unlikely to
provide the investor with much additional knowledge of
the security, i.e., with much predictive ability. For example, it is very cheap to employ the following strategy: "If
the security goes up today, I'll buy tomorrow." Since this
strategy only involves looking at someone else's newspaper
and making a telephone call, we would expect it to earn
practically nothing. Computing serial correlation coefficients of past price changes and using them as a basis for
prediction is more expensive than buying a newspaper, but
it is cheap enough to preclude the hope of a large income
gain. In fact, any temporal statistical dependence in the
univariate price change series for a single security is easy
to detect today with the aid of surplus computer time.
This is one reason the random walk hypothesis of stock
market prices enjoys empirical success. There should be
very little dependence between successive price changes
of a particular security because the past price of that
security is one of the cheapest and most obvious variables
to monitor.[1]

A variable can follow a strict random walk with respect
to its own sequence and still be successfully predicted. For
instance, let the price of a security in period t be completely determined by

$$p_t = p_{t-1} + e_t$$

where the "random" disturbance term, e, is given by

$$e_t = u_{t-1}$$

Here, u_{t-1} is some random variable which is independent and identically distributed over time but is *observable* one period earlier than t. The price change, $p_t - p_{t-1}$, is completely independent of past price changes and yet completely predictable by u.

Of course, there is no known variable such as u that bears a deterministic lagged relation to real security price changes. In major securities markets, there are thousands of random variables and events whose information contents are continuously evaluated by thousands of market participants. Probably none of these are deterministically related to market price, but the basic principle of marginal productivity still applies to their evaluation even though its precise working is difficult to perceive in an environment of such complex uncertainty.

THE EFFICIENT MARKET MODEL

The model used in the rest of this book is an idealized securities market where all information is reflected in current market prices. The model assumes:

1. Zero transactions costs.
2. Symmetric market rationality (a concept due to Miller and Modigliani [1961, pp. 427-428]), which means that every trader acts rationally (i.e., desires more wealth and uses all available information) and believes others do likewise.
3. Information is free and becomes available to everyone at the same instant.

These conditions are sufficient to assure that no trading rule is profitable in the accounting sense.[2] The reason for this follows: If all available information about the future earnings of a security is not accounted for, the present worth of future earnings (value) will not be equal to price. A discrepancy between price and value is an opportunity for profitable trading that rational investors will act upon.

Since no available information is neglected in this efficient market, the only possible reason for changing one's estimate of value is the receipt of *unanticipated* information. Hence, value will be expected to remain unchanged from one period to the next, and, since price is an unbiased estimate of value in every period, price also will be expected to remain unchanged. Algebraically,

$$E_{t-1}(\tilde{p}_t^d \mid B_{t-1}) = p_{t-1} \qquad (2\text{-}1)$$

where E_{t-1} is the mathematical expectations operator as of period $t-1$, and $\tilde{p}_t^d$ is the discounted present value in $t-1$ of the price (including interest or dividend accruals) of the security in period t. (This price is, of course, a random variable in $t-1$ and hence is surmounted by a tilde.) B_{t-1} represents all available information about the security's value in $t-1$, and p_{t-1} is the observed market price in $t-1$.

Since $\tilde{p}_t^d$ is a discounted present value of the market price in t as of $t-1$, there exists a continuously compounded discount rate, ρ_{t-1}, such that $p_t^d \exp(\rho_{t-1}) = p_t$, where p_t is the market price in t. Thus (2-1) may be written in terms of market price as[3]

$$E_{t-1}(\tilde{p}_t \mid B_{t-1}) = p_{t-1} \exp(\rho_{t-1}) \qquad (2\text{-}2)$$

Generally, ρ_{t-1} is thought to be nonnegative. Consequently,

$$E_{t-1}(\tilde{p}_t \mid B_{t-1}) \geqslant p_{t-1} \qquad (2\text{-}3)$$

Furthermore, since B_{t-1} *represents* all available information in $t-1$, it includes all the past market prices, p_{t-1}, $p_{t-2}, \ldots, p_0$, and (2-3) can be written

$$E_{t-1}(\tilde{p}_t \mid B_{t-1}, p_0, \ldots, p_{t-1}) \geqslant p_{t-1} \qquad (2\text{-}4)$$

Expression (2-4) is the classic statement of a submartingale sequence in p. As such, it shares all the important characteristics of the statistical theory of martingales. Many of these statistical properties will be used in the sequel, both for theoretical proofs and for empirical testing, and they will be discussed in detail at that time.

Upon comparing this result to the random walk model mentioned in Chapter 1, the reader will discover that the present model is less restrictive. The random walk model assumes that the disturbance term, $U_{j,t}$ (cf. p. 3), is independently and identically distributed through time. The submartingale model makes no assumption about the disturbance term other than that its expectation exists.[4]

IMPLICATIONS OF THE MODEL FOR TRADING PRACTICES

The Impossibility of Systems[5]

We shall now show that when market price follows a submartingale sequence,

$$E_{t-1}(\widetilde{p}_t) = \exp(\rho_{t-1})p_{t-1}^{\,6} \qquad (2\text{-}5)$$

no system based on past information can earn more than the normal market return, ρ_{t-1}, on average.

Let ϵ_{t-1} be a B_{t-1} measurable[7] random variable assuming only the values zero and one. Suppose that when $\epsilon_{t-1} = 1$, the investor buys n shares at the end of period $t-1$, and that when $\epsilon_{t-1} = 0$, he buys none.[8] The particular value of ϵ_{t-1}, either zero or one each period, is the output of the investor's "system." Hence, ϵ_{t-1} is a true random variable at the beginning of $t-1$ since the system may depend on probabilistically affected exogenous events.

Since the number of shares the investor holds during period t is denoted by n, his change in wealth, W, from $t-1$ to t is given by the sum of $\epsilon_{t-1}n(p_t - p_{t-1})$ for the shares he buys and

$$[\exp(\rho_{t-1}) - 1](W_{t-1} - \epsilon_{t-1}np_{t-1})$$

for the competitive market return he is able to earn on that portion of his wealth not invested in shares; i.e.,

$$W_t - W_{t-1} = \epsilon_{t-1}n(p_t - p_{t-1}) + [\exp(\rho_{t-1}) - 1](W_{t-1} - \epsilon_{t-1}np_{t-1})$$

As of $t-1$, W_{t-1}, ϵ_{t-1}, p_{t-1}, and ρ_{t-1} are nonstochastic. Thus, taking expectations of both sides as of $t-1$ provides

$$E_{t-1}(\widetilde{W}_t) - W_{t-1} = \epsilon_{t-1}n[E_{t-1}(\widetilde{p}_t) - p_{t-1}]$$
$$+ [\exp(\rho_{t-1}) - 1](W_{t-1} - \epsilon_{t-1}np_{t-1})$$

From equation (2-5), however, the difference $E_{t-1}(p_t) - p_{t-1} = p_{t-1}[\exp(\rho_{t-1}) - 1]$, and the wealth change equation reduces to

$$E_{t-1}(\widetilde{W}_t) = W_{t-1} \exp(\rho_{t-1}) \qquad (2\text{-}6)$$

Equation (2-6) shows that, on average, the return derived from *any* trading system based on past information is precisely the market return, ρ_{t-1}. Note that a "successful" system is defined by

$$E_{t-1}(\widetilde{W}_t) > \exp(\rho_{t-1})W_{t-1}.$$

NOTES

1. In the absence of a market that anticipates the future, the serial dependence in natural events such as rainfall or dividend declarations would be passed on to market price. In the case of a perishable commodity such as a cantaloupe, market price changes are, in fact, serially dependent. But the price of a perfectly indestructible commodity such as a security behaves much differently because traders can obtain an advantage by advance discounting of the serial dependence in earnings, dividends, taxes, etc.

2. In reality, of course, none of these assumptions is absolutely valid, and we observe that some trading rules earn revenue. However, as we argued in the first part of this chapter, competition will drive *economic* profit to zero even when transactions costs exist and information is not free.

3. $\exp(x)$ means e^x, where $e \doteq 2.718$ is the base of natural logarithms. Continuous compounding is due to the following property:

Let

$$\left(1 + \frac{r}{b}\right)^{nb}$$

be the discount factor when r is rate of return per period, n is the number of periods, and b is the number of compounding intervals per period. As the number of compounding intervals increases without bound, we have

$$\lim_{b \to \infty} \left(1 + \frac{r}{b}\right)^{nb} = e^{nr}$$

4. The disturbance term U is not an explicit part of equation (2-2) but is implied by the expectations operator. It could take any one of a variety of forms, such as multiplicative, $p_t = p_{t-1} \exp(\rho_{t-1} + U_t)$; additive, $p_t = p_{t-1} \exp(\rho_{t-1}) + U_t$; combination, $p_t = p_{t-1} \exp(\rho_{t-1} + U_{1,t}) + U_{2,t}$; etc.; provided that (2-4) holds.

HUNT LIBRARY
CARNEGIE-MELLON UNIVERSITY

5. This proof is adapted from Feller (1966, p.213).

6. The conditional notation will be dropped when no confusion is possible, but E_{t-1} should be understood as an expectation conditional on B_{t-1}.

7. Saying that ϵ_t is B_{t-1} measurable means that it cannot depend upon knowledge of the future.

8. The possibility of short sales is ignored. The proof would still work if short sales were permitted, but it would be unnecessarily complicated. We assume that the investor earns a normal return ρ_{t-1}, from a savings account, say, during the periods when he does not buy.

Chapter 3

Equilibrium Interest Rates
in an Efficient Market

This chapter derives the static and dynamic equilibrium conditions for interest rates (or, more precisely, for internal rates of return) in an efficient bond market. First, several definitions and algebraic relations to be used many times later are given. Then a rough dynamic equilibrium equation is derived from the submartingale formulation of Chapter 2. Finally, a general equilibrium theory of the term structure is used to obtain the basic results.

INTEREST RATE RELATIONS

The market price of a fixed-maturity, noncoupon bond with n periods to maturity as of period t is denoted $p_{n,t}$. *Both* subscripts change with calendar time so that a *given* bond has the following price sequence (it has N periods to maturity in the issuing period T):

$$(p_{N,T}, p_{N-1,T+1}, p_{N-2,T+2}, \cdots, p_{0,N+T})$$

$p_{0,N+T}$ is the (known) maturity value.

The Yield to Maturity

The yield to maturity, or simply the yield, is defined as the *continuously compounded internal rate of return* at which the future income stream of the bond must be discounted to equal the current price. For a bond with a maturity value of $1, no coupon payments, and n periods to maturity as of period t, the market price and the yield as of t are related by

$$p_{n,t} = \exp(-nR_{n,t}) \text{ dollars} \qquad (3\text{-}1)$$

where the yield, $R_{n,t}$, is in units of (percentage per period)/100.

The Forward Rate

A yield to maturity over n periods can be thought of as a sequence of n one-period yields. For continuous compounding, the forward rate, $r_{j,t}$, which is the *one-period yield* that is supposed to start $j - 1$ periods after the start of period t, is related to the yield to maturity by

$$R_{n,t} = (r_{1,t} + r_{2,t} + \cdots + r_{n,t})/n \qquad (3\text{-}2)$$

Simple algebra with equation (3-2) provides the definition of the forward rate in terms of yields,

$$r_{n,t} = nR_{n,t} - (n - 1)R_{n-1,t} \qquad (3\text{-}3)$$

The importance of forward rates is due to their economic interpretation, viz., the forward rate is the marginal return obtained by committing the investment for one additional period.

The Yield Curve

A set of yields to maturity, all observed on the same calendar date, may be regarded as a function of time to maturity. The actual function (usually fitted by least squares or simply by plotting the yields on the vertical axis of a graph and the time to maturity on the horizontal axis and then fitting a freehand curve) is called the *yield curve* or the *term structure of interest rates.*

A SIMPLE MARTINGALE FORMULATION FOR YIELD SEQUENCES

In terms of noncoupon bond prices, the efficient market equation (2-5) is

$$E_{t-1}(\widetilde{p}_{n,t}) = \exp(\rho_{n,t-1})p_{n+1,t-1} \qquad (3\text{-}4)$$

Note that $\rho_{n,t-1}$ is an *unknown* discount rate for the bond. It is not necessarily equal to $R_{n,t}$ or any other associated yield or forward rate.

The definitional equation (3-1) can be written

$$nR_{n,t} = -\log_e(p_{n,t})$$

which shows that $nR_{n,t}$ is a convex function of $p_{n,t}$.

Taking logarithms of both sides of (3-4) provides

$$-\log_e E_{t-1}(\widetilde{p}_{n,t}) = -\rho_{n,t-1} - \log_e(p_{n+1,t-1})$$

Applying Jensen's inequality (Feller, 1966, pp. 151-152) and the definition of yields provides

$$E_{t-1}(n\widetilde{R}_{n,t}) \geqslant (n+1)R_{n+1,t-1} - \rho_{n,t-1}$$

or equivalently

$$E_{t-1}(\widetilde{R}_{n,t}) \geq R_{n+1,t-1} + \frac{1}{n}(R_{n+1,t-1} - \rho_{n,t-1}) \qquad (3\text{-}5)$$

Expression (3-5) is one form of the fundamental dynamic equation for interest rates in an efficient market. It is a logical result of the assumptions of the efficient market model and has required no additional knowledge. However, it is a deficient expression for several reasons: First, it is an inequality; second, $\rho_{n,t-1}$ is undetermined; third, due to the first two faults, it is not testable. To make it testable, we now enlist the aid of term structure theory.

THE TERM STRUCTURE APPROACH TO A DYNAMIC EXPRESSION FOR INTEREST RATES IN AN EFFICIENT MARKET

Static Equilibrium in the Loan Market

According to Hicks (1946, pp. 144-145), "if we decide upon some minimum period of time, loans for less than which time we shall be prepared to disregard, every loan of every duration can be reduced to a standard pattern—a loan for the minimum period, combined with a given number of renewals for subsequent periods of the same length, contracted forward."

We may think of an n-period loan as having a current yield of $R_{n,t}$ or as being a loan for Hicks' minimum period (with yield $R_{1,t}$), plus $n-1$ forward loans (each renewal j having as a current yield the forward rate, $r_{j,t}$).

It is natural to compare the forward rate with a corresponding future one-period spot yield. Consider the result of a transaction in which a trader issues an $(n-1)$-period bond and buys an n-period bond in period t. After $(n-1)$

periods, the bond he originally issued matures and he becomes a net lender holding a one-period bond. If the one one-period yield then, $R_{1,t+n-1}$, is greater than

$$nR_{n,t} - (n-1)R_{n-1,t} \equiv r_{n,t},$$

he would have earned a higher return if he had made no transaction at all in period t but had waited and bought the one-period bond at $t + n - 1$. In general, if investor i, who wishes to have a net lending position at time $t + n - 1$, has an expectation in t, $E^i_t(\tilde{R}_{1,t+n-1}) > r_{n,t}$, and a linear utility function, he will not make the forward transaction but will wait and buy the one-period bond later. If, on the other hand, he is a risk averter, he will make the forward transaction (which has a certain return for the future period equal to $r_{n,t}$) unless $E^i_t(\tilde{R}_{1,t+n-1})$ is sufficiently larger than $r_{n,t}$ to induce him to accept its associated risk.

In this discussion of forward rates we have intended to show the crucial fact that an investor's behavior toward loans of any maturity can be deduced from his behavior toward forward loans. We are now prepared to derive the expression for an equilibrium term structure.

Begin by assuming that:

1. Every trader i possesses subjective probability distributions on future one-period spot rates from the present period t up to and including period $t + N - 1$.
2. Interest rates for periods $t + N$ and on are of no concern to anyone (i.e., everyone has an investment horizon less than or equal to N).
3. Bonds are completely free of default risk.
4. As of t, each trader i has an excess demand function

for forward loans corresponding to each future period j up to and including $t + N - 1$, given by

$$q_{j,t}^i = f_j^i(r_{1,t} - {}_jr_{1,t}^i;\ r_{2,t} - {}_jr_{2,t}^i;\ \dots\ ;\ r_{N,t} - {}_jr_{N,t}^i) \qquad j = 1, 2, \dots, N$$

Here, $q_{j,t}^i$ is the demand as of t, by trader i, for one-period forward loans applicable to period $t + j - 1$ ($q_{j,t}^i$ is positive for lending and negative for borrowing); $r_{k,t}$ is the one-period market forward rate for k periods hence, i.e., *from now*, observed in t, and the numbers ${}_jr_{1,t}^i,\ {}_jr_{2,t}^i,\ \dots,\ {}_jr_{N,t}^i$ are chosen such that

$$q_{j,t}^i = f_j^i(0, 0, \dots) = 0$$

That is, the numbers ${}_jr_{1,t}^i,\ {}_jr_{2,t}^i,\ \dots$ are the personal forward rates of trader i. If each of the market forward rates happened to be exactly equal to its corresponding personal rate, trader i would have zero excess demand for j-period forward loans.

Each personal forward rate ${}_jr_{k,t}^i$ is dependent on four quantities:

1. Trader i's current expectation about the one-period spot rate in $t + k - 1$
2. The degree of confidence trader i has in this expectation
3. Trader i's degree of risk aversion
4. The maturity preference he has about the future period, $t + k - 1$, i.e., his current assessment of the amount of spot borrowing or lending he would undertake in $t + k - 1$ if his expectation on $R_{1,t+k-1}$ were realized

We assume that these four quantities can be expressed in an additive form by the typical equation

$$_jr^i_{k,t} = {_jL^i_{k,t}} + E^i_t(\widetilde{R}_{1,t+k-1} \mid B^i_t)$$

for $j = 1, 2, \ldots, N$ and $k = 1, 2, \ldots, N$, where $_jL^i_{k,t}$ is a risk and maturity premium, $E^i_t(\widetilde{R}_{1,t+k-1} \mid B^i_t)$ is trader i's expected one-period spot rate for period $t + k - 1$ as of period t, and B^i_t represents trader i's information in t.[1]

Characteristics of the Excess Demand Formulation

Consider the case $k = j$:

$$_jL^i_{j,t} = {_jr^i_{j,t}} - E^i_t(\widetilde{R}_{1,t+j-1} \mid B^i_t)$$

Now $_jL^i_{j,t}$ will be positive under the following conditions[2]: (1) trader i is a risk averter, and (2) if the expected future spot rate were to be realized exactly, i.e., if

$$R_{1,t+j-1} = E^i_t(\widetilde{R}_{1,t+j-1} \mid B^i_t)$$

then trader i would be a spot borrower in $t + j - 1$. This is because, as a risk averter, trader i is willing to pay something additional now to obtain the certain borrowing rate, $r_{j,t}$, rather than risk having to pay a higher rate at $t + j - 1$. Conversely, $_jL^i_{j,t}$ will be negative if trader i is a risk averter and would be a spot lender in $t + j - 1$ if his expectation were realized. He would be willing to give up some return now in order to get the certain rate, $r_{j,t}$. Also, the more confidence trader i has in his expectation, the smaller $_jL^i_{j,t}$ must be. As he becomes more confident, he is willing to sacrifice less in order to avoid the risk.

The basic idea of this theory is that forward loan demand curves are derived from demand curves for corresponding future spot loans. Figure 3-1 illustrates this for the case of

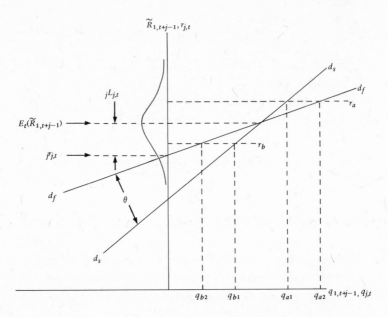

FIGURE 3-1   Excess Demand Functions for Spot and Forward Loans

a risk-averting trader who is certain about all future incomes earned outside the capital markets. The two demand curves are $d_f d_f$ for forward loans, $q_{j,t}$, and $d_s d_s$ for spot loans, $q_{1,t+j-1}$. The curves cross at $E_t(\widetilde{R}_{1,t+j-1} \mid B_t)$, the mean of the probability distribution on $\widetilde{R}_{1,t+j-1}$, because:

1. At a forward rate r_a the trader will make forward loans of at least q_{a1}, since he would make spot loans of this amount in $t + j - 1$ if $R_{1,t+j-1}$ were certain (r_a is certain). This means that $d_f d_f$ will never be to the left of $d_s d_s$ when $r_{j,t} > E_t(\widetilde{R}_{1,t+j-1} \mid B_t)$. In fact, $d_f d_f$ will be to the right of $d_s d_s$ at a rate such as r_a since the trader will also loan $q_{a2} - q_{a1}$ for speculative

reasons. He will liquidate these speculative loans (the $q_{a2} - q_{a1}$) at the beginning of $t + j - 1$ and obtain a capital gain whose expected return in t is $r_a - E_t(\widetilde{R}_{1,t+j-1} \mid B_t)$.

2. At the rate $r_b < E_t(\widetilde{R}_{1,t+j-1} \mid B_t)$, the trader will only make loans of $q_{b\,2}$. He will hope to obtain a higher return on the spot market in $t + j - 1$ and will postpone his transactions for $q_{b1} - q_{b2}$ until it appears certain that the spot rate in $t + j - 1$ will be no higher than r_b.

At forward rates lower than $_jr_{j,t}$, the trader will borrow forward. This is equivalent to a forward short sale. The trader will exercise his borrowing option (sell the securities short) at the beginning of period t and will cover the sale by purchases at the lower price (higher spot rate) he now (in t) expects will prevail in $t + j - 1$.

The trader's forecasting confidence affects the angle θ between $d_s d_s$ and $d_f d_f$. For example, if the trader were absolutely certain that his expectation would prevail [i.e., if the entire probability mass were located at $E_t(\widetilde{R}_{1,t+j-1} \mid B_t)$], then $d_f d_f$ would be horizontal. At current forward rates just greater or less than $E_t(\widetilde{R}_{1,t+j-1} \mid B_t)$, the trader could obtain what he regarded as *certain* capital gains, and he would arbitrage by lending or borrowing until the forward rate returned to $E_t(\widetilde{R}_{1,t+j-1} \mid B_t)$. Conversely, the greater the uncertainty about $\widetilde{R}_{1,t+j-1}$, the smaller the angle must be between $d_f d_f$ and $d_s d_s$. The limiting case, when the trader has a "diffuse" distribution on $\widetilde{R}_{1,t+j-1}$, would show $d_f d_f$ and $d_s d_s$ coincidental. The trader would be so uncertain that he would simply make the same amount of forward loans in t as he would have made spot loans in $t + j - 1$

at the same market interest rate. He would not speculate on capital gains.

The angle θ is also influenced by the trader's degree of risk aversion. A risk-indifferent trader will have a horizontal $d_f d_f$ since his rule is to maximize *expected* gain. The more risk averse the trader, the smaller θ will be until the coincidental case is reached where the trader is so risk averse that no amount of expected capital gain will make him speculate. The forward loan excess demand curve of a risk preferrer *may* be negatively sloped. We at least know that at market rates such as $r_a > E_t(\widetilde{R}_{1,t+j-1} \mid B_t)$, $d_f d_f$ would lie to the left of $d_s d_s$ and vice versa for rates such as $r_b < E_t(R_{1,t+j-1} \mid B_t)$. At the certain rate r_a, for example, the risk preferrer would make fewer forward loans than q_{a1}, choosing to give up some expected return for the gain of uncertainty.

Two factors exogenous to this system also influence $_j L_{j,t}$ and $_j r_{j,t}$ indirectly by their effect on $d_s d_s$. These are the resources of the trader and his consumption-saving plans in $t + j - 1$. Clearly, the greater the trader's resources, the flatter $d_s d_s$ (and hence $d_f d_f$) will be. Time preferences are reflected in the level of $d_s d_s$. Consider the demand functions of two individuals b and l, who have identical expectations on $\widetilde{R}_{1,t+j-1}$ and similar confidence levels but who differ in that trader b has a strong desire to consume more than his income during $t + j - 1$ and trader l has a strong desire to consume less; i.e., at a spot rate equal to their expectation, trader b would be a borrower and trader l a lender in $t + j - 1$. Their excess demand functions might look something like Figure 3-2. Although these traders have identical expectations and similar risk preference functions, $_j L_{j,t}^l < 0$ and $_j L_{j,t}^b > 0$ and consequently $_j r_{j,t}^l < _j r_{j,t}^b$. The points where the demand curves intersect the $r_{j,t}$ axis are by definition the personal forward rates, that is, the values of the market forward rate at which no forward borrowing or lending occurs.

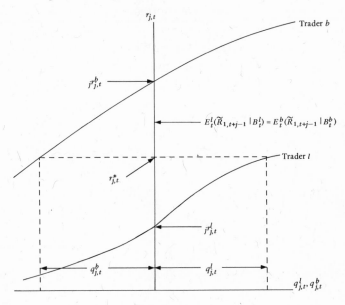

FIGURE 3-2   Excess Demand Functions of Two Traders Who Are Similar in Every Respect Except Their Propensity to Consume During $t+j-1$.

Since the slope of each demand function also depends on the trader's resources, if b and l constituted the entire market and l had more resources, his demand curve would be flatter, other things being equal. Consequently, the market rate they would agree upon (using a tâtonnement process) would be $r_{j,t}^*$, where $-q_{j,t}^b = q_{j,t}^l$ in Figure 3-2, a rate considerably lower than the expectation. Trader b would not only obtain the certain rate $r_{j,t}^*$ but would actually obtain a surplus over the riskier expectation.

Demand functions in terms of forward loans are mathematically more tractable than demand functions for bonds, and they are used here for that reason. One should remember, however, that the two approaches are equivalent. The demand function for any bond can be written as a suitable combination of forward loan demands; viz., the demand as of t by trader i for n-period bonds, $Q_{n,t}^i$, is

$$Q_{n,t}^i = q_{n,t}^i - q_{n+1,t}^i {}^3$$

in terms of forward loan demands.

Just as the excess demand function for forward loans is written in terms of forward rates, the excess demand function for n-period bonds can be written in terms of yields as

$$Q_{n,t}^i = q_{n,t}^i - q_{n+1,t}^i = F_n^i(R_{1,t} - {}_nR_{1,t}^i, R_{2,t} - {}_nR_{2,t}^i, \ldots)$$

where

$$R_{n,t} = \sum_{j=1}^{n} \frac{r_{j,t}}{n}$$

and

$$_nR_{j,t}^i = \sum_{k=1}^{j} \frac{[{}_nL_{k,t}^i + E_t^i(\widetilde{R}_{1,t+k-1})]}{n}$$

MARKET EQUILIBRIUM

To obtain an approximate solution for the equilibrium term structure, we expand each excess demand function in a Maclaurin series. Recalling that $q(0, 0, \ldots, 0) = 0$, this results in

$$q_{j,t}^i = (r_{1,t} - {}_jr_{1,t}^i)\frac{\partial f_j^i}{\partial R_1} + \sum_{k=2}^{N} [r_{k,t} - E_t^i(\widetilde{R}_{1,t+k-1}) - {}_jL_{k,t}^i]\frac{\partial f_j^i}{\partial r_{k,t}}$$

$$+ \text{ higher-order terms in } r \qquad (3\text{-}6)$$

the partial derivatives being taken at the points

$$r_{k,t} = {}_jr_{k,t}^i$$

Each investor will have N excess demand functions such as (3-6) which can be written in vector[4] notation as

$$(\mathbf{q}_t^i)' = (q_{1,t}^i : \cdots : q_{n,t}^i)$$

We can also define the vectors

$$(\mathbf{r}_t)' = (r_{1,t} : \cdots : r_{N,t})$$

$$_k\mathbf{r}_t^i = ({}_kr_{1,t}^i : \cdots : {}_kr_{N,t}^i)$$

where, of course, ${}_kr_{j,t}^i = {}_kL_{j,t}^i + E_t^i(\widetilde{R}_{1,t+j-1})$ and thus ${}_k\mathbf{r}_t^i$ $= [R_{1,t} : E_t^i(\widetilde{R}_{1,t+1}) : \cdots : E_t^i(\widetilde{R}_{1,t+N-1})] + ({}_kL_{1,t}^i : \cdots : {}_kL_{N,t}^i) \equiv \mathbf{E}_t^i + {}_k\mathbf{L}_t^i$, and the matrix

$$\mathbf{F}^i \equiv \begin{bmatrix} \partial f_1^i/\partial r_{1,t} \cdots \partial f_1^i/\partial r_{N,t} \\ \\ \\ \\ \\ \partial f_N^i/\partial r_{1,t} \qquad \partial f_N^i/\partial r_{N,t} \end{bmatrix}$$

Denoting the kth row of $\mathbf{F}^i$ by $\mathbf{F}_k^i$, the system of N excess demand functions is expressed as

$$\mathbf{q}_t^i = \mathbf{F}^i \mathbf{r}_t - \boldsymbol{\phi}_t^i + \text{higher-order terms}$$

where $\boldsymbol{\phi}_t^i$ is an $N \times 1$ column vector whose kth element is

$$_k \mathbf{r}_t^i (\mathbf{F}_k^i)'$$

The market equilibrium is the set of forward rates for which the total excess demand is zero; i.e.,

$$\sum_i \mathbf{q}_t^i = 0$$

If the higher-order terms are neglected,[5] a solution is given by

$$\sum_i (\mathbf{F}^i \mathbf{r}_t - \boldsymbol{\phi}_t^i) = 0$$

or

$$\mathbf{r}_t = \sum_i \; [(\sum_i \mathbf{F}^i)^{-1} \boldsymbol{\phi}_t^i] \qquad (3\text{-}7)$$

To elucidate this basic result, let us suppose for a moment that all the cross-elasticities of demand are zero, i.e., that $\mathbf{F}^i$ has nonzero elements only on the diagonal. In this case, the equilibrium k-period forward rate is given by

$$r_{k,t} = \sum_i \left\{ \left(\frac{W_i}{\sum_i W_i} \right) [E_t^i(\widetilde{R}_{i,t+k-1}) + {}_k L_{k,t}^i] \right\} \qquad (3\text{-}8)$$

where $W_i = \partial f_k^i / \partial r_{k,t}$.

This shows that $r_{k,t}$ is a weighted-average expectation over all traders in the market, the weights depending on:

1. Investor resources: W_i measures the amount of bonds demanded per unit change in rates. Clearly, this will be larger the wealthier the trader.
2. Investor confidence in expectations coupled with maturity preference,

$$| _kL^i_{k,t} | = | _kr^i_{k,t} - E^i_t(\widetilde{R}_{1,t+k-1}) |$$

will be larger the less confident trader i is about his expectation. The sign of $_kL^i_{k,t}$ will depend on whether i is in the borrowing or lending portion of his excess demand curve at $r_{k,t}$. The forward rate $r_{k,t}$ will be a biased high estimate of the future one-period spot rate if (a) wealthier traders tend to be borrowers; or (b) lenders are more confident about their expectations; or (c) borrowers are more risk averse than lenders; or (d) at a value for $r_{k,t}$ equal to the average (across traders) expectation on $\widetilde{R}_{1,t+k-1}$, there are more borrowers than lenders (a net positive excess demand for borrowing).[6]

Finally, we mention that the special solution (3-8) is exactly the same as the results derived by Bierwag and Grove (1967) under a stricter set of assumptions. They consider a two-period model where the trader is always a net lender and find quite properly that $r_{2,t}$ is "a weighted-average of investor's predicted rates," each weight varying directly with the size of his investment fund, his ability to bear risk, and his confidence in expectations (p. 52).

A NOTATIONAL SIMPLIFICATION

The off-diagonal elements of F^i will not usually be zero [although they should often be a maximum along the diagonal and decline (in absolute value) away from it]. Consequently, the equilibrium forward rates will be very complex weighted averages. The rate $r_{k,t}$ will depend on:

1. The vector E_t^i of one-period rates expected by each trader
2. Each trader's risk premium vector $_k L_t^i$
3. The entire matrix F^i of each trader

And even this complicated result is only an approximation, albeit a good one, because all second- and higher-order terms have been dropped from the Maclaurin expansion.

To simplify the analysis, we shall now extract individual equations from the system. Equation (3-7) can be rewritten

$$r_t = \sum_i \left\{ \left(\sum_i F^i \right)^{-1} \begin{bmatrix} (_1 L_t^i + E_t^i)(F_1^i)' \\ \cdot \\ \cdot \\ \cdot \\ \cdot \\ \cdot \\ \cdot \\ \cdot \\ \cdot \\ \cdot \\ (_N L_t^i + E_t^i)(F_N^i) \end{bmatrix} \right\}$$

Let $\mathbf{X}_t^i$ be the N-element column vector whose jth element is the jth *diagonal* element of

$$\begin{bmatrix} {}_1\mathbf{L}_t^i \\ {}^{..} \\ {}^{.} \\ {}^{.} \\ {}^{.} \\ {}^{..} \\ {}_N\mathbf{L}_t^i \end{bmatrix} (\mathbf{F}^i)' \equiv \mathbf{L}_t^i(\mathbf{F}^i)'$$

Then

$$\mathbf{r}_t = \sum_i \left\{ \left(\sum_i \mathbf{F}^i \right)^{-1} \mathbf{F}^i \left[(\mathbf{F}^i)^{-1}\mathbf{X}_t^i + (\mathbf{E}_t^i)' \right] \right\}$$

The matrix $\mathbf{v}^i \equiv \left(\sum_i \mathbf{F}^i \right)^{-1} \mathbf{F}^i$ is a measure of the wealth and maturity preferences of trader i relative to the wealth and maturity preferences of all traders.

Denoting the kth row of $\mathbf{v}^i$ as $\mathbf{v}_k^i$ and $\mathbf{v}_k^i$'s jth element as $\mathbf{v}_{kj}^i$, then

$$r_{k,t} = \sum_i \mathbf{v}_k^i(\mathbf{E}_t^i)' + \sum_i \mathbf{v}_k^i(\mathbf{F}^i)^{-1}\mathbf{X}_t^i$$

$$= \sum_i \mathbf{v}_{kk}^i \mathbf{E}_t^i(\widetilde{R}_{1,t+k-1}) + L_{k,t}$$

where

$$L_{k,t} = \sum_i [\mathbf{v}_k^i(\mathbf{F}^i)^{-1}\mathbf{X}_t^i + \mathbf{v}_k^i(\mathbf{E}_t^i)' - \mathbf{v}_{kk}^i \mathbf{E}_t^i(\widetilde{R}_{1,t+k-1})] \quad (3\text{-}9)$$

Thus

$$r_{k,t} = E_t(\widetilde{R}_{1,t+k-1}) + L_{k,t} \quad (3\text{-}10)$$

$E_t(\widetilde{R}_{1,t+k-1})$ being a weighted-average expectation over all traders.

In term structure literature, $L_{k,t}$ is called the "liquidity premium." From (3-9) it is obviously no simple function of risk or maturity preference and, in fact, involves all expectations on future one-period rates, the entire matrix L_t^i, and the cross-sectional distribution of investor wealth.

The equilibrium term structure defined by (3-10) is a fundamental result and one which we will use extensively. It is well to keep its complex nature in mind.

THE DYNAMIC MARKET EQUATION

In the preceding sections, a static equilibrium equation (3-10) for forward rates was derived. It contains quantities $E_t(\widetilde{R}_{1,t+k-1})$ and $L_{k,t}$, which are averages of individual expectations and behavioral quantities. Recall that each individual expectation is conditioned by the trader's state of knowledge as of t, B_t^i. Similarly, the *weighted-average* expectation should be conditioned by $B_t = \cup_i B_t^i$. The union of sets notation is used because the true conditioning variable for the market *is* a combination (or union) of individual information, much of which is common to all individuals.

The presence of the expectations operator implies the existence of a probability density function, $dP(R_{1,t+j} \mid B_t)$, such that

$$E_t(\widetilde{R}_{1,t+j} \mid B_t) = \int_{-\infty}^{\infty} R_{1,t+j}\, dP\,(R_{1,t+j} \mid B_t) \qquad (3\text{-}11)$$

(This does not necessarily suggest that points on the distribution function are averages weighted across all traders with the same weights as the expectations.)

Given the existence of such distributions for all maturities, it can be shown (Roll, 1968, pp. 28-29), using a proof given by Samuelson (1965, p. 45), that in an efficient market the variable

$$x_{j,t} \equiv r_{j,t} - L_{j,t}$$

follows the pure martingale sequence

$$(x_{j,t}, x_{j-1,t+1}, \dots)$$

That is,

$$E_{t-1}(\tilde{r}_{j,t} - \tilde{L}_{j,t} \mid B_{t-1}) = r_{j+1,t-1} - L_{j+1} \qquad (3\text{-}12)$$

Equation (3-12) is the fundamental dynamic equation for an efficient loan market. It will hold irrespective of the behavior of traders toward maturity since their attitudes are captured in the liquidity premium, L. It states that the forward rate applicable to a fixed future calendar date, less a liquidity premium, follows a martingale sequence. There is no presumption that the variability of the forward rate is constant over time or that the error implied by the expectation operator is serially independent, uncorrelated with $r_{j+1,t-1} - L_{j+1,t-1}$, or described by any specific probability law.

The result is in terms of forward rates but the behavioral equation for any yield or price can be obtained by a simple combination of the forward rate equations. All such equations are testable provided that a measure of the L's can be obtained. These measures are given by the various hypotheses of the term structure which are described in Chapter 4.

NOTES

1. B_t^i is defined such that it does *not* contain knowledge of the current market equilibrium rates ($r_{k,t}$) but does contain all other relevant information available to trader i. (The current market rates are to be determined by the interaction of all traders and implicitly by the interaction of their information states; i.e., a tâtonnement process determines equilibrium and each observed market rate is an equilibrium rate.)

2. When considering this case, all other market forward rates are assumed equal to their corresponding "personal rates" (i.e., $r_{k,t} = {}_jr_{k,t}^i$ for $k \neq j$).

3. The demand for n-period forward loans is equal to the total demand for bonds of n periods *or more* to maturity; i.e.,

$$q_{n,t}^i = \sum_{\tau=0}^{\infty} Q_{n+\tau,t}^i$$

Thus,

$$q_{n,t}^i - q_{n+1,t}^i = \sum_{\tau=0}^{\infty} Q_{n+\tau,t}^i - \sum_{\tau=0}^{\infty} Q_{n+\tau+1,t}^i = Q_{n,t}^i$$

4. Vectors and matrices are denoted by boldface letters.

5. The higher-order terms *will* be small under many believable distributions of investors. The quantities $\mathbf{E}_t^i$ and $\mathbf{L}_t^i$ probably have roughly bell-shaped distributions *across traders*—$\mathbf{E}_t^i$ because it involves the *same* body of economic knowledge processed differently by each i and $\mathbf{L}_t^i$ because most people are thought to conform to a norm of risk and maturity preference. Fewer and fewer people deviate farther and farther from the norm.

If $\mathbf{E}_t^i$ and $\mathbf{L}_t^i$ *are* roughly bell-shaped across i and if the equilibrium is reached near their modes, quadratic terms such as $(r_{j,t} - {}_jr_{j,t}^i)^2$ and similar higher-than-quadratic terms will be very small and $r_{j,t}$ will be close to ${}_jr_{j,t}$ in *most* cases. Terms such as $(r_{j,t} - {}_jr_{k,t}^i)^2$, which may be large when $|k - j|$ is large, will have little effect because their associated partial derivative weights $\partial^2 f_{j,t}/(\partial_j r_{k,t}^i)^2$ will be typically small.

6. This is the reason Hicks gives for the "liquidity-preference hypothesis" of the term structure (1946, pp. 146-447), when he states that there is a "constitutional weakness" on the lending side of the market that becomes more pronounced with increasing maturity.

Chapter 4

Hypotheses of the Term
Structure of Interest Rates

Chapter 3 derived the fundamental dynamic equation for interest rates in an efficient market,

$$E_{t-1}(\widetilde{r}_{j,t} - \widetilde{L}_{j,t} \mid B_{t-1}) = r_{j+1,t-1} - L_{j+1,t-1} \qquad (3\text{-}12)$$

where $r_{j,t}$ is the one-period forward rate for j periods hence, observed in period t, and $L_{j,t}$ is the j-period liquidity premium observed in period t. As indicated by this equation, the quantity $X_{j,t} \equiv r_{j,t} - L_{j,t}$ follows a pure martingale sequence; i.e.,

$$E_{t-1}(\widetilde{X}_{j,t}) = X_{j+1,t-1}; E_{t-2}(\widetilde{X}_{j+1,t-1}) = X_{j+2,t-2}; \text{etc.}$$

But the martingale property is testable only if all variables in the sequence are observable, and liquidity premiums cannot be obtained directly. One can, however, estimate them from other (observable) variables by relying on implications of the several term structure hypotheses. The task of the present chapter is to describe these hypotheses and to use their implications for transforming (3-12) into a testable equation.

Since each term structure hypothesis implies something different about L, we shall obtain several alternative and competing testable forms of the basic equation (3-12). These can be used to perform discriminatory tests of term structure hypotheses in addition to the basic test of efficiency [i.e., the test of (3-12)].

THE PURE EXPECTATIONS HYPOTHESIS

This hypothesis, associated with Lutz (1940-1941) and Meiselman (1962), asserts that the L's are identically zero for all j and t. Meiselman does not argue that preference for maturity is entirely nonexistent but only that "as a matter of descriptive reality . . . speculators who are *indifferent to uncertainty* will bulk sufficiently large to determine market rates on the basis of their *mathematical expectations alone*" (p. 10) (italics inserted).

With $L_{j,t} = 0$ for all j and t, equation (3-12) can be written

$$E_{t-1}(\widetilde{r}_{j,t} \mid B_{t-1}) = r_{j+1,t-1} \qquad (4\text{-}1)$$

which describes a pure martingale process for the forward rate sequence.

Movement of the Yield Curve

Using the definition of forward rates and equation (4-1),

$$nE_{t-1}(\widetilde{R}_{n,t} \mid B_{t-1}) = \sum_{j=1}^{n} E_{t-1}(\widetilde{r}_{j,t} \mid B_{t-1}) = \sum_{j=1}^{n} r_{j+1,t-1}$$

$$= (n+1)R_{n+1,t-1} - r_{1,t-1} \qquad (4\text{-}2)$$

$$E_{t-1}(\widetilde{R}_{n,t} \mid B_{t-1}) = R_{n+1,t-1} + \frac{1}{n}(R_{n+1,t-1} - R_{1,t-1}) \quad (4\text{-}3)$$

The reader may easily determine the implications of equation (4-3) for movement of the yield curve over time. Only a flat yield curve has the same expected shape next period. Yield curves with any other shape will tend to change shapes from period to period.

Movement of Market Prices

Equation (4-2) can be recast in terms of the market price, $p_{n,t} \equiv \exp(-nR_{n,t})$, as

$$E_{t-1}[\log(\tilde{p}_{n,t}) \mid B_{t-1}] = \log[p_{n+1,t-1} \exp(r_{1,t-1})] \qquad (4\text{-}4)$$

Equation (4-4) provides information about two matters: First, the log price follows a martingale sequence if it is adjusted for the interest accrual factor [which under this hypothesis is $\exp(r_{1,t-1})$]. If the log price is not adjusted in this manner, the serial correlation in the price *relatives* or in the log *first differences* will be high because it will depend on the serial correlation in the one-period interest rate *level*.[1] Second, the expected log price relative is

$$E_{t-1}[\log_e(\tilde{p}_{n,t}/p_{n+1,t-1}) \mid B_{t-1}] = r_{1,t-1}$$

If the pure expectations hypothesis is correct, the expected return from holding any default-free bond for one period is the current short term rate *and* is completely independent of the maturity of the bond. This result might have been expected. The pure expectations hypothesis assumes that investors are indifferent to risk associated with maturity, and, if the risks on all bonds are equal, the expected returns must be equal over any holding period.

THE MARKET SEGMENTATION HYPOTHESIS

The basic premise of the market segmentation hypothesis is *securities of different maturities are imperfect substitutes*. Some of the L's are nonzero. Preferences for certain maturities occur because fixed-payment securities are used as hedges against the payment streams of assets or liabilities that must be held in the course of business but which entail risks of interest rate fluctuations that businessmen do not care to incur. No other assertions have been made by the hypothesis. If the hypothesis is to be tested, some additional assumptions and implications must be added to and drawn from the basic theory. The next two subsections develop two variants of the hypothesis based on observed maturity preference patterns of investors.

The Time-Dependent Variant

The time-dependent variant is based on the following observation: The maturities of the payment streams of many assets and liabilities depend on calendar time. For example, a railroad may finance a locomotive (whose useful life is predictable and finite) by issuing a bond whose duration matches the locomotive's life expectancy. Since the life of the locomotive declines with calendar time, the railroad has a maturity habitat which declines at least partially with calendar time.

If individuals with calendar-time-dependent maturity habitats *dominate the market*, $L_{n,t}$ should be about equal to $L_{n+1,t-1}$ aside from (1) random changes due to unexpected shifts in some individuals' maturity preferences and (2) systematic changes that reflect a decrease in uncertainty about the expected future one-period yield as the date when it starts draws nearer.

In a simple algebraic model to fulfill these requirements and describe the hypothesis, the random change can be indicated by an expectations operator; i.e.,

$$E_{t-1}(\widetilde{L}_{j,t}) = L_{j+1,t-1} + g(.)$$

The function g and its arguments should be chosen such that the decreasing riskiness (due to decreasing maturity) is measured properly. To satisfy the latter requirement, we choose

$$g(.) = R_{j,t-1} - R_{j+1,t-1} + a_j \qquad (4\text{-}5)$$

where a_j is an arbitrary constant. Equation (4-5) constitutes an assumption that the "systematic" change in liquidity premiums between $t - 1$ and t is a linear function of a current (in $t - 1$), differential between adjacent yields.

The total model of the time-dependent market segmentation hypothesis is thus

$$E_{t-1}(\widetilde{L}_{j,t}) = L_{j+1,t-1} + R_{j,t-1} - R_{j+1,t-1} + a_j \qquad (4\text{-}6)$$

[Please note that equation (4-6) is an assumption of the hypothesis analogous to the assumption made by the pure expectations hypothesis that all the L's are zero.]

Equation (4-6) can be used to simplify the fundamental dynamic equation of efficient loan markets to

$$E_{t-1}(\widetilde{r}_{j,t}) = r_{j+1,t-1} + a_j + R_{j,t-1} - R_{j+1,t-1} \qquad (4\text{-}7)$$

Now, instead of the forward rate being a pure martingale

sequence (as it was under the pure expectations hypothesis), the forward rate first difference will be serially correlated if there is serial dependence in the yield difference, $R_{j,t-1} - R_{j+1,t-1}$. The yield difference *will* be serially dependent if the yield curve tends to retain the same shape over long periods, and there is considerable evidence that the shape of the yield curve *does* persist (see, e.g., Figure 5-2).

MOVEMENT OF YIELDS

A dynamic equation for yield movements is simply derived by summing (4-7) over j:

$$\sum_{j=1}^{n} E_{t-1}(\tilde{r}_{j,t}) = \sum_{j=1}^{n} (r_{j+1,t-1} + a_j + R_{j,t-1} - R_{j+1,t-1})$$

or

$$E_{t-1}(n\tilde{R}_{n,t}) = R_{1,t-1} - R_{n+1,t-1} + \sum_{j=1}^{n} (r_{j+1,t-1} + a_j)$$

Defining $nA_n = \sum_{j=1}^{n} (a_j)$, we have

$$E_{t-1}(n\tilde{R}_{n,t}) = nA_n + (n+1)R_{n+1,t-1} - R_{1,t-1} + R_{1,t-1} - R_{n+1,t-1}$$

$$E_{t-1}(\tilde{R}_{n,t}) = A_n + R_{n+1,t-1} \qquad (4\text{-}8)$$

The simplicity of (4-8) is a partial justification for the particular assumptions made in stating the algebraic model of this hypothesis. The result (4-8) is a submartingale in the sequence

$$(R_{n+1,t-1}, R_{n,t}, R_{n-1,t+1}, \ldots)$$

MOVEMENT OF PRICES

Using the familiar relation between yields and prices, equation (4-8) can be manipulated to result in

$$E_{t-1}[\log_e(\tilde{p}_{n,t}/p_{n+1,t-1})] = (R_{n+1,t-1} - nA_n) \qquad (4\text{-}9)$$

Since nA_n is a constant by assumption, the log price relative will be serially uncorrelated if it is first adjusted by a yield with the same maturity as the maturity of the price in the relative's denominator. This contrasts with the result for the pure expectations hypothesis that the price relative should be adjusted by the *one-period* yield in all cases.

The Stationary Variant

The stationary variant of the market segmentation hypothesis is based on the observation that some asset and liability payment streams are independent of calendar time, retaining approximately the same maturity by being periodically renewed. This situation might occur when a firm uses many similar assets, each with a small unit value, whose individual failure rates are predictable. For example, a telephone company could finance each home telephone with, say, a $10 installment loan that has a maturity equal to the average length of time home phones are retained. The user's periodic payments would satisfy the installments and thus result in an adequate hedge between the phone's income and the loan. On an individual basis, the loans would decline in maturity with calendar time, but for the telephone company as a whole the aggregate loan used to finance all home phones should have a stationary matu-

rity (since new subscribers are constantly replacing cancella-
tions), approximately equal to the expected failure rate of
the equipment.

It should not be surprising to learn that stationary (in
calendar time) hedging behavior is common even among
firms which hold a wide variety of dissimilar assets. Many
companies maintain "lines of credit" or periodically renew-
able loans with banks. These really amount to bonds with
fixed maturities.

If such behavior dominates the loan market, the liquidity
premium $L_{j,t}$ should be about equal to $L_{j,t-1}$ (the liquidity
premium for the same maturity one period earlier), except
for random shifts in the types of investors who participate
in the market and shifts in these participants' maturity
preferences; i.e.,

$$E_{t-1}(\widetilde{L}_{j,t}) = L_{j,t-1} \qquad (4\text{-}10)$$

Equation (4-10) constitutes the assumption of the model
we shall use to describe this hypothesis. Substituting (4-10)
into the fundamental equation (3-1) results in

$$E_{t-1}(\widetilde{r}_{j,t}) = r_{j+1,t-1} + L_{j,t-1} - L_{j+1,t-1} \qquad (4\text{-}11)$$

Again, the forward rate is no longer a pure martingale
and the serial dependence in forward rate changes could
be substantial if the difference in adjacent liquidity premiums, $L_{j,t-1} - L_{j+1,t-1}$, changes slowly over time.

MOVEMENTS OF YIELDS

Summing (4-11) over j results in

$$E_{t-1}(n\widetilde{R}_{n,t}) = \sum_{j=1}^{n} (r_{j+1,t-1}) - L_{n+1,t-1} \qquad (4\text{-}12)$$

Here, the fact that $L_{1,t-1} = 0$ was utilized.[2]

This equation can be rearranged to yield

$$E_{t-1}(\widetilde{R}_{n,t}) = R_{n,t-1} + \frac{1}{n}(r_{n+1,t-1} - R_{1,t-1} - L_{n+1,t-1}) \quad (4\text{-}13)$$

From (3-10) we note that

$$r_{n+1,t-1} - L_{n+1,t-1} = E_{t-1}(\widetilde{R}_{1,t+n-1})$$

and hence,

$$E_{t-1}(\widetilde{R}_{n,t}) = R_{n,t-1} + \frac{1}{n}[E_{t-1}(\widetilde{R}_{1,t+n-1}) - R_{1,t-1}] \quad (4\text{-}14)$$

Equation (4-14) is a testable equation. *If* the one-period yield sequence $(R_{1,t}, R_{1,t+1}, \ldots)$ is a submartingale, then $E_{t-1}(\widetilde{R}_{1,t+j} - R_{1,t-1})$ is a constant and all sequences such as $(R_{n,t}, R_{n,t+1}, \ldots)$ for $n > 1$ will also be submartingales. If the one-period yield sequence is not a submartingale, none of the sequences in higher-maturity yields will be submartingales. In fact, the serial dependence in all yield changes such as $R_{n,t} - R_{n,t-1}$ will be proportional to serial dependence in one-period yield changes.

PRICE MOVEMENTS

Equation (4-12) can be utilized directly to express the price relative. The result is

$$E_{t-1}[\log(\widetilde{p}_{n,t}/p_{n+1,t-1})] = (R_{1,t-1} + L_{n+1,t-1}) \quad (4\text{-}15)$$

This result contrasts to the pure expectations hypothesis only by the addition of $L_{n+1,t-1}$ to the interest accrual factor $(R_{1,t-1} + L_{n+1,t-1})$. When the log price relative is adjusted by this factor, it will be serially uncorrelated.

THE LIQUIDITY PREFERENCE HYPOTHESIS

This hypothesis is a refinement of what we have called the stationary variant of the market segmentation hypothesis. It was first suggested by Hicks (1946, pp. 146-147), who presumed that "if no extra return is offered for long lending, most people (and institutions) would prefer to lend short . . . ."[3] This idea has been developed more completely by others. Kessel (1965, p. 44) argues that "forward rates are biased and high estimates of future short-term rates," i.e., that *the L's are all positive*, and that "since the risk of capital losses attributable to holding securities is directly related to term to maturity, security yields ought also to vary directly with maturity" (p. 45), i.e., *that the L's increase monotonically with n.*[4]

Since the L's are supposed to vary with n and not necessarily with t, this hypothesis is a refined version of the stationary variant of the market segmentation hypothesis. The two hypotheses can be distinguished only in an ambiguous way by average liquidity premiums (which can be computed from the data; cf. Table 6-12). The liquidity preference hypothesis predicts that average liquidity premiums will increase monotonically with maturity, but such a result is also *consistent* with (although not predicted by) the stationary market segmentation hypothesis.

Otherwise, the two hypotheses are not distinguishable, and we shall henceforth combine them. The dynamic behavioral equations (4-11), (4-14), and (4-15) for forward rates, yields, and prices apply to the liquidity preference hypothesis as well as to the stationary market segmentation hypothesis.

NOTES

1. The interest rate level is serially correlated even if changes in the level are not.

2. From equation (3-10) for $k = 1$, $E_{t-1}(\widetilde{R}_{1,t-1}) = r_{1,t-1} - L_{1,t-1}$. But $r_{1,t-1} = R_{1,t-1}$, and in $t-1$, $E_{t-1}(R_{1,t-1}) = R_{1,t-1} = r_{1,t-1}$. Hence $L_{1,t-1} = 0$.

3. He argued that borrowers were maturity indifferent.

4. There is another reason short-term yields might be lower. Short-term bonds are presumably good money substitutes. Consequently, some of their total return may be nonpecuniary and attributable to the utility one ordinarily derives from holding cash. To this extent, the pecuniary return on short-term bonds can be correspondingly lower. For a persistent long-short yield differential, however, an additional requirement is necessary; viz., long-term bonds must be *poorer* money substitutes than short-term bonds. This requirement evidently means that the market for long-term bonds has to be more imperfect (due to higher transactions costs, thinness, etc.) than the market for short-term bonds.

Chapter 5

Description of the Data

The data are internal rates of return on U.S. Treasury bills. Treasury bills are the shortest-term debt obligations of the federal government. Since bills have no coupon payments, they sell at a discount from the maturity price, and the pecuniary return is due solely to price appreciation.

The sample consists of 796 weekly yield curve observations from October 1946 through December 1964. From October 1949 through February 1959, the treasury normally issued 91-day bills only (i.e., bills with 91 days or 13 weeks to maturity upon issuance). During this period, there are 13 bill yield observations each week, 1 observation for the new 91-day issue and 12 observations for old bills ranging from 1 to 12 weeks in maturity. Beginning in March 1959, 26 bill yield observations are available each week (ranging in maturity from 7 to 182 days). During this later period, the treasury issued new bills of both 182 days and 91 days to maturity.

INSTITUTIONAL CHARACTERISTICS OF THE BILL MARKET

The keystone of the government bill market is a group of dealers, numbering about nineteen at present, who maintain inventories of bills for their own accounts, bid on new bills, and buy and sell outstanding bills.[1]

Auctions of new bills are conducted weekly. The treasury accepts competitive bids from the dealers and from others whom the dealers advise (U.S. Congress, p. 3). It supposedly acts as a perfectly discriminating monopolist, tapping the demand curve from the top until the intended quantity is sold. Noncompetitive bids are accepted for amounts equal to or less than $200,000, and these are filled at the average price of the competitive bids.

Outstanding bills are traded in an "over-the-counter" market. The dealers are prepared at any time to make bid or ask quotations on the basis of a "banker's discount" yield. The price to the buyer or seller is computed from the banker's discount yield (always quoted in percent per 360 days) as follows: Let R_n^b be a banker's discount yield for a bill with n days to maturity. The price of a $100 (at maturity) bill as of now is

$$p_n = 100 - \frac{n}{360} R_n^b$$

For purposes of testing, the banker's discount yields were converted to true rates of return, compounding continuously, by the formula

$$R_n = -(36{,}500/n) \log_e(p_n/100)$$

where R_n is the true rate of return in percent per annum.

The peculiarities of the market concerning sale and delivery are as follows: First, bills always mature on Thursdays except when Thursday is a legal holiday in which case they mature on the following Friday. (A list of legal holidays

TABLE 5-1   Legal Holidays and Years During the Sample Period
             When the Holiday Occurred on Tuesday, Wednesday,
             or Thursday

Holiday	Tuesday	Wednesday	Thursday
New Year's Day, Jan. 1	1952, 1957, 1963	1958, 1964	1953, 1959
Lincoln's birthday, Feb. 12	1952, 1957, 1963	1958, 1964	1953, 1959
Washington's birthday, Feb. 22	1949, 1955	1950, 1956, 1961	1951, 1962
Memorial Day, May 30	1950, 1961	1951, 1956, 1962	1957, 1963
Independence Day, July 4	1950, 1961	1951, 1956, 1962	1957, 1963
Columbus Day, Oct. 12	1954	1949, 1955, 1960	1950, 1961
Election Day[a]	All years	—	—
Armistice Day, Nov. 11	1952, 1958	1953, 1959, 1964	1954
Thanksgiving Day[b]	—	—	All years
Christmas Day, Dec. 25	1951, 1956, 1962	1957, 1963	1952, 1958

[a]First Tuesday after first Monday in November.
[b]Fourth Thursday in November.

during the sample period is given in Table 5-1.) Second, there is a lag of two *working* days between sale and delivery. (However, the quotations and sales are made on the basis of delivery date, not sale date.) As a consequence, quotations for bills with an even number of weeks to maturity are usually made on Tuesdays because two working days later, when the bill is delivered and paid for, is a Thursday. The data sample consists primarily of Tuesday closing quotations so that the maturities are for even weeks.

Holidays which fall on Tuesday, Wednesday, or Thursday cause problems. If the holiday is on Tuesday, no quotes are made, but the Monday quotes are for even weeks since there are two working days from Monday to Thursday. When a holiday occurs on Wednesday, the Tuesday quotes are not for an even number of weeks because delivery is postponed until Friday. However, the Monday quotes are for bills deliverable on the following Thursday and are thus for even weeks. In both cases, when a holiday falls on Tuesday or Wednesday, the Monday quotes are used here. Thursday holidays cause more serious problems because for 13 or 26 weeks before the maturity date, the bill that eventually matures on the Friday after a Thursday holiday does not have an even number of weeks to maturity in the Tuesday quotations.

Holidays are disturbing because they introduce measurement error into the data. First, tests based on term to maturity should be careful about interest rates associated with Thursday holidays because these observations are not for even weeks until maturity. Tests based on lagged observations should carefully examine interest rates associated with Tuesday or Wednesday holidays because the Monday quotations are made 6 days from the preceding and 8 days from the following Tuesday instead of 7 days from each.

To determine the effects of holidays, and to eliminate as much measurement error as possible, every test that follows was conducted with two sample sets—with and without the holiday-associated observations. No significant difference was observed in the two sets of results. Only the complete sample results are reported hereafter. Results based on omitting holiday-associated observations are reported in Roll (1968).

TABLE 5-2   Reproduction of U.S. Treasury Bill Quote Card,
             Merrill Lynch, Pierce, Fenner & Smith, Government
             Securities Division, January 31, 1967

U.S. TREASURY BILLS

Amt. Out.	Maturity	Days	—Bid—		—Asked—		Equivalent Bond Yield
2.3	2/9/67	7	4.40%	99.914	4.10%	99.920	4.16%
2.3	2/16/67	14	4.50%	99.825	4.25%	99.835	4.32%
2.3	2/23/67	21	4.50%	99.738	4.35%	99.746	4.42%
1.0	2/28/67	26	4.50%	99.675	4.30%	99.689	4.37%
2.3	3/2/67	28	4.55%	99.646	4.40%	99.658	4.48%
2.3	3/9/67	35	4.55%	99.558	4.45%	99.567	4.53%
2.3	3/16/67	42	4.55%	99.469	4.45%	99.481	4.54%
2.0	3/22/67[a]	48	4.52%	99.397	4.42%	99.411	4.51%
	Yld 3/15				5.17%		
2.3	3/23/67	49	4.56%	99.879	4.46%	99.393	4.55%
2.3	3/30/67	56	4.56%	99.291	4.46%	99.306	4.55%
1.4	3/31/67	57	4.56%	99.278	4.46%	99.294	4.55%
2.3	4/6/67	63	4.54%	99.206	4.46%	99.220	4.56%
2.3	4/13/67	70	4.54%	99.117	4.46%	99.133	4.56%
2.3	4/20/67	77	4.54%	99.029	4.46%	99.046	4.57%
2.5	4/21/67[a]	78	4.54%	99.016	4.46%	99.034	4.57%
	Yld 4/15				4.83%		
2.3	4/27/67	84	4.54%	98.941	4.46%	98.959	4.57%
1.4	4/30/67	87	4.54%	98.903	4.46%	98.922	4.57%
2.3	5/4/67	91	4.52%	98.857	4.47%	98.870	4.58%
1.0	5/11/67	98	4.54%	98.764	4.48%	98.780	4.60%

Continued on following page

METHODS OF DATA FILTERING

Banker's discount yields were punched and verified
directly from dealer quote cards.[2] The cards were taken
from the files of the Chicago office of Merrill Lynch,
Pierce, Fenner & Smith, Government Securities Division

TABLE 5-2 (continued)

U.S. TREASURY BILLS

Amt. Out.	Maturity	Days	—Bid—		—Asked—		Equivalent Bond Yield
1.0	5/18/67	105	4.54%	98.676	4.48%	98.693	4.60%
1.0	5/25/67	112	4.54%	98.588	4.48%	98.606	4.61%
1.4	5/31/67	118	4.56%	98.505	4.50%	98.525	4.63%
1.0	6/1/67	119	4.56%	98.493	4.50%	98.513	4.63%
1.0	6/8/67	126	4.56%	98.404	4.50%	98.425	4.64%
1.0	6/15/67	133	4.56%	98.315	4.50%	98.338	4.64%
2.8	6/22/67[a]	140	4.56%	98.227	4.50%	98.250	4.64%
	Yld 6/15				4.74%		
1.0	6/22/67	140	4.56%	98.227	4.50%	98.250	4.64%
1.0	6/29/67	147	4.56%	98.138	4.50%	98.163	4.65%
1.5	6/30/67	148	4.54%	98.134	4.48%	98.158	4.63%
1.0	7/6/67	154	4.56%	98.049	4.50%	98.075	4.65%
1.0	7/13/67	161	4.56%	97.961	4.50%	97.988	4.66%
1.0	7/20/67	168	4.56%	97.872	4.50%	97.900	4.66%
1.0	7/27/67	175	4.54%	97.793	4.48%	97.822	4.64%
1.5	7/31/67	179	4.52%	97.753	4.46%	97.782	4.62%
1.0	8/3/67	182	4.50%	97.725	4.45%	97.750	4.61%
1.5	8/31/67	210	4.52%	97.363	4.46%	97.398	4.63%
1.4	9/30/67	240	4.52%	96.987	4.46%	97.027	4.63%
1.4	10/31/67	271	4.52%	96.597	4.46%	96.643	4.64%
0.9	11/30/67	301	4.52%	96.221	4.46%	96.271	4.65%
0.9	12/31/67	332	4.46%	95.887	4.40%	95.942	4.61%
0.9	1/31/68	363	4.46%	95.503	4.40%	95.563	4.62%

Yields for Delivery, February 2, 1967

[a]Tax Anticipation Series.

Closing Quotations, Tuesday, January 31, 1967

(formerly C. J. Devine & Company). A reproduction of one such card is given in Table 5-2.[3]

These data were passed through a series of filtering programs whose purposes were:

1. Date validity. The programs checked that:

      a. Each date was in sequence.

      b. Each date was a Tuesday (except when Tuesday or Wednesday was a holiday in which case the date was Monday).

  2. Rate validity. The following events caused the quotation to be checked:

      a. Bid yield less than ask yield

      b. Negative forward rate

      c. Change in rates with same maturity, $|R_{n,t} - R_{n,t-1}|$, abnormally large

      d. Change in forward rates, $|r_{n,t} - r_{n+1,t-1}|$, abnormally large

      e. Change in rates for a given bill, $|R_{n,t} - R_{n+1,t-1}|$, abnormally large

      f. Bid-asked yield spread abnormally large or small

      g. Residuals from a Meiselman regression, $|u_t| = |r_{n,t} - r_{n+1,t-1} - \hat{a} - \hat{b}(r_{1,t} - r_{2,t-1})|$, abnormally large[4]

Each offending quotation was checked for keypunching error and for agreement between the banker's discount rate and the price on the quote card. A total of 3 keypunching errors and 13 quote card errors was found.

HISTORICAL STATISTICS

One-week bid-ask average yields are plotted against time in Figure 5-1. The very smooth section in 1949 and 1950 is before the famous Treasury-Federal Reserve "accord" of March 1951. Before the accord, the Federal Reserve System used open market operations to peg interest rates on bills and maintain a government securities yield curve of a certain shape (Friedman and Schwartz, 1963, pp. 620-627).

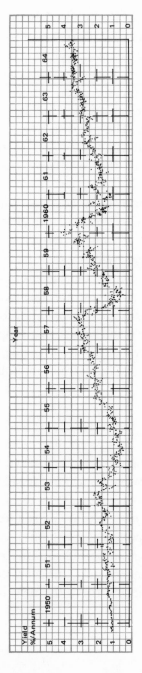

FIGURE 5-1. One-Week Yields, Bid-Asked Averages, U.S. Treasury Bills, October 1949–December 1964

Mean *bid* yields for five subperiods are plotted as average yield curves in Figure 5-2. Corresponding average bid-asked spreads are plotted below the yield curves. These data are tabulated in Table 5-3, which also provides (1) the mean asked quotations for the same subperiods, (2) the semi-interquartile range[5] corresponding to each mean, and (3) the sample sizes. The subperiods were chosen to provide roughly equal-sized samples subject to the natural cutoff of March 1959 when the yield curve was lengthened from 13 to 26 weeks.

These statistics provide several bits of information. First, in each of the five subperiods, the yield curve is upward sloping on average. Second, contrary to popular opinion, short-term yields generally show just as much variation as long-term yields. Third, the bid-ask yield spread has a peculiar shape. It is largest for one-week bills, declines evenly with maturity to 12 weeks, drops sharply from 12 to 13 weeks, and in the last two subperiods (when the 14- through 26-week yields are available) rises from 13 to 14 weeks and then again declines monotonically from 14 to 26 weeks.

The large spread for short-term bills is easily explained. Dealers profit by the bid-asked spread in *prices*, and a small price spread on a very short-term bill results in an enormous spread between bid and asked yields. For example, a ½-cent price spread on a 7-day, $100 bill will result in a yield spread of about .25 percent per annum. The same price spread on a 91-day bill results in a yield spread of only about .02 percent per annum.

The sharp change in spreads around new issue dates is not so easy to understand. One view contends that the market has trouble absorbing the new issues of 13-week

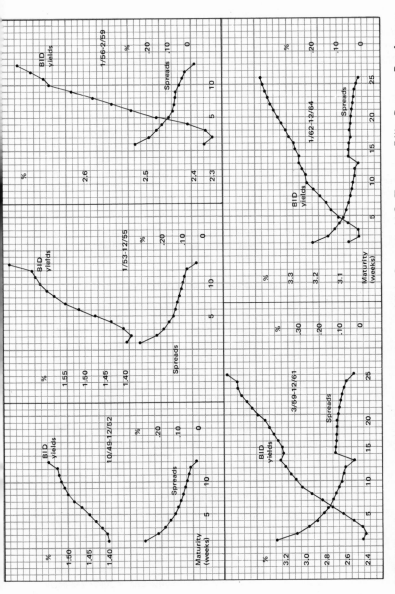

FIGURE 5-2. Average Yield Curves and Average Yield Spreads, U.S. Treasury Bills, Percent Per Annum

TABLE 5-3   Average Yield Curves, 1949-1964, U.S. Treasury Bills

Maturity (weeks)	Mean Bid	S.I.Q. Range[a] Bid	Mean Asked	S.I.Q. Range Asked	Mean Spread	S.I.Q. Range Spread	Sample Size
October 1949-December 1952							
1	1.412	.213	1.205	.207	.2068	.0710	170
2	1.415	.188	1.245	.183	.1700	.0510	170
3	1.425	.213	1.279	.163	.1461	.0455	170
4	1.434	.203	1.304	.178	.1296	.0305	170
5	1.444	.213	1.330	.203	.1146	.0305	170
6	1.458	.223	1.354	.213	.1034	.0255	170
7	1.469	.233	1.373	.223	.0950	.0155	170
8	1.478	.223	1.390	.233	.0879	.0205	170
9	1.484	.238	1.404	.233	.0801	.0200	170
10	1.490	.238	1.415	.244	.0748	.0105	170
11	1.493	.238	1.423	.239	.0704	.0150	170
12	1.497	.238	1.432	.234	.0640	.0155	170
13	1.512	.249	1.465	.239	.0472	.0055	158
January 1953-December 1955							
1	1.382	.406	1.153	.431	.2292	.0260	156
2	1.374	.431	1.197	.431	.1762	.0255	156
3	1.387	.431	1.239	.457	.1481	.0260	156
4	1.409	.431	1.275	.431	.1337	.0255	156
5	1.434	.431	1.314	.457	.1199	.0205	156
6	1.458	.467	1.346	.467	.1126	.0005	156
7	1.482	.467	1.377	.457	.1050	.0005	156
8	1.499	.477	1.400	.477	.0985	.0105	156
9	1.514	.487	1.421	.487	.0936	.0105	156
10	1.523	.487	1.436	.487	.0870	.0100	156
11	1.530	.487	1.447	.482	.0828	.0100	156
12	1.537	.482	1.464	.477	.0732	.0100	156
13	1.572	.492	1.522	.492	.0498	.0095	152
January 1956-February 1959							
1	2.309	.558	2.070	.558	.2391	.0260	165
2	2.295	.543	2.102	.583	.1932	.0255	165
3	2.305	.518	2.141	.533	.1640	.0255	165
4	2.337	.467	2.194	.457	.1436	.0250	165
5	2.382	.421	2.256	.431	.1262	.0255	165

Continued on following page

TABLE 5-3 (continued)

Maturity (weeks)	Mean Bid	S.I.Q. Range[a] Bid	Mean Asked	S.I.Q. Range Asked	Mean Spread	S.I.Q. Range Spread	Sample Size
			January 1956-February 1959				
6	2.422	.447	2.305	.457	.1169	.0255	165
7	2.452	.457	2.342	.441	.1107	.0005	165
8	2.486	.416	2.380	.431	.1068	.0005	165
9	2.518	.406	2.418	.406	.1007	.0005	165
10	2.550	.406	2.455	.406	.0952	.0105	165
11	2.567	.396	2.478	.406	.0887	.0105	165
12	2.581	.386	2.504	.386	.0777	.0105	165
13	2.608	.401	2.561	.630	.0471	.0055	155
			March 1959-December 1961				
1	2.440	.532	2.148	.457	.2922	.0760	148
2	2.428	.456	2.198	.456	.2294	.0510	148
3	2.451	.436	2.256	.406	.1944	.0505	148
4	2.500	.416	2.332	.431	.1680	.0505	148
5	2.574	.401	2.427	.401	.1468	.0505	148
6	2.644	.431	2.515	.431	.1281	.0255	148
7	2.706	.416	2.593	.406	.1138	.0005	148
8	2.763	.437	2.659	.431	.1039	.0005	148
9	2.821	.452	2.724	.426	.0969	.0105	148
10	2.867	.467	2.777	.457	.0899	.0105	148
11	2.899	.477	2.814	.467	.0850	.0200	148
12	2.923	.487	2.848	.467	.0757	.0200	148
13	2.965	.497	2.914	.497	.0508	.0050	148
14	2.950	.462	2.841	.457	.1092	.0005	148
15	2.955	.452	2.847	.457	.1082	.0005	148
16	2.978	.432	2.870	.432	.1078	.0005	148
17	3.005	.417	2.899	.411	.1064	.0005	148
18	3.033	.427	2.928	.401	.1047	.0005	148
19	3.069	.417	2.967	.416	.1022	.0005	148
20	3.107	.432	3.008	.407	.0991	.0005	148
21	3.141	.457	3.044	.447	.0964	.0100	148
22	3.177	.478	3.083	.467	.0934	.0105	148
23	3.208	.528	3.118	.528	.0900	.0105	148
24	3.232	.544	3.151	.539	.0815	.0200	148
25	3.259	.570	3.186	.559	.0728	.0105	148
26	3.288	.569	3.237	.584	.0515	.0100	144

Continued on following page

TABLE 5-3 (continued)

Maturity (weeks)	Mean Bid	S.I.Q. Range[a] Bid	Mean Asked	S.I.Q. Range Asked	Mean Spread	S.I.Q. Range Spread	Sample Size
			January 1962-December 1964				
1	3.067	.401	2.889	.360	.1783	.0255	157
2	3.037	.376	2.911	.370	.1260	.0255	157
3	3.039	.355	2.934	.340	.1054	.0105	157
4	3.063	.355	2.971	.345	.0919	.0100	157
5	3.095	.345	3.015	.355	.0794	.0200	157
6	3.118	.345	3.046	.350	.0721	.0150	157
7	3.137	.335	3.071	.350	.0662	.0150	157
8	3.156	.340	3.096	.340	.0599	.0155	157
9	3.178	.330	3.123	.340	.0549	.0100	157
10	3.192	.330	3.142	.340	.0502	.0095	157
11	3.200	.330	3.154	.340	.0460	.0055	157
12	3.209	.335	3.167	.340	.0414	.0095	157
13	3.220	.335	3.186	.341	.0345	.0050	157
14	3.221	.325	3.161	.345	.0608	.0150	157
15	3.229	.330	3.168	.335	.0603	.0155	157
16	3.238	.340	3.178	.345	.0599	.0155	157
17	3.249	.335	3.190	.350	.0594	.0150	157
18	3.260	.341	3.201	.351	.0587	.0155	157
19	3.273	.335	3.216	.351	.0568	.0055	157
20	3.284	.345	3.230	.351	.0547	.0095	157
21	3.297	.346	3.245	.351	.0517	.0095	157
22	3.307	.351	3.257	.351	.0499	.0050	157
23	3.316	.351	3.269	.356	.0475	.0055	157
24	3.325	.356	3.281	.361	.0437	.0100	157
25	3.332	.351	3.293	.361	.0391	.0095	157
26	3.340	.351	3.308	.356	.0318	.0005	148

[a]S.I.Q. Range = semi-interquartile range.

bills (which usually trebles the total amount outstanding), i.e., that there is a downward-sloping demand curve for 13-week bills (with total quantity of bills outstanding being measured on the horizontal axis).

Some people have trouble digesting this view and propose an alternative, viz., that the dealers collude to offer the government a low price on its new issues. This is supported by the fact that the spread drops suddenly from 12 to 13 weeks and from 25 to 26 weeks. If the market absorption theory were correct, the decrease in spread would be smoother.

Another possible alternative involves dealer costs. There are about three times as many bills of 13 weeks or less as there are bills of 14 through 26 weeks in maturity. Consequently, the 1-13-week bill market is probably much more active than the 14-26 week market. To the extent that that this is true, the brokerage function of the dealers would cost less because it would be easier to find buyers and sellers. Inventories could also be maintained at a lower level since dealers could increase or decrease them more easily. The lower cost of the brokerage service is reflected by a lower price, i.e., by a generally smaller yield spread. This argument explains the upward shift of the entire curve from 14 to 26 weeks but it fails to explain the sharp drops from 12 to 13 and from 25 to 26 weeks.

Another possibility, suggested by Prof. Kessel, is supported by the bid-asked *price* spreads plotted in Figure 5-3. (We have previously been examining yield spreads.) As he suggests, these data indicate that the spread pattern results from a combination of two factors: First, dealers have very short-term maturity preferences, consider long-term bills more risky to hold in inventory than short-term bills, and therefore charge a higher price for dealing in long-term bills. Second, the market is much more active around new issue maturities (i.e., 13 and 26 weeks). As argued above, dealers are able to operate at a lower per unit cost in more active markets and they consequently charge a lower price. The result is a general rise in price spreads with maturity

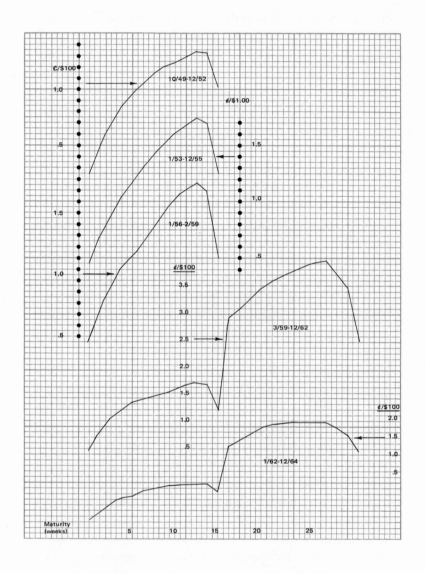

FIGURE 5-3.   Average Price Spreads, U.S. Treasury Bills

due to the increasing inventory risk except around 13 and 26 weeks where the risk is offset by a much more active market. That the new issue market actually *is* more active than the market at other maturities is supported by the previously cited U.S. Congressional study of the dealer market (1960). That study provides evidence that "sales of new bills by the dealers have accounted for roughly 20 to 25 per cent of their total sales of bills" (p. 55). This indicates that the trading volume at 13 and 26 weeks is very much larger than the volume at any other maturity.

If Kessel's explanation is correct, we can observe from Figure 5-3 that the trading volume is also relatively large at maturities just less than the new issue maturities. This is indicated by the downturns in the curves at 12 and 24-25 weeks. Such evidence is quite plausible. One might expect investors to take a week or more to settle their portfolio adjustments after a large flotation of new securities. During this time, the dealers would be busy.

NOTES

1. A comprehensive description of dealer activities is provided by the U.S. Congress, Joint Economic Committee (1960). It is interesting to note that the government securities dealers handle a dollar volume about five times as large as the volume of the New York Stock Exchange (p. 68).

2. Quote cards are lists of the daily closing quotations (banker's discount yields and their corresponding prices) and are published by many of the dealers and mailed to their customers.

3. In Table 5-2, the regular weekly treasury issues have the days to maturity italicized. Other issues are either "tax anticipation" series or end-of-month series. Only the regular issues were used here.

Under the "bid" and "asked" headings, two numbers appear. The first is the bankers' discount yield in percentage per 360 days. The second is price as a percentage of maturity value.

4. In each test based on outliers, *abnormal* is defined as being outside the middle 95 percent of the ordered sample values.

5. The semi-interquartile range is one-half the difference between the 75th and 25th sample percentiles.

Chapter 6

Empirical Tests

Data described in Chapter 5 will be used here to perform two types of tests: (1) tests that discriminate among theories of the term structure and (2) tests of bill market efficiency. Our goal is to find the term structure hypothesis that fits the data best and to use its implications in market efficiency tests.

One of the testing methods to be used relies on knowledge of the probability distributions of the variables. It will therefore be necessary to check the empirical distributions of the variables to be tested for conformance to known probability laws. Then we shall discuss (1) the appropriate methods for testing a variable for martingale behavior and (2) statistical inference and measures of scale when the distributions are members of the stable class. Finally, the empirical results will be tabulated and discussed.

EMPIRICAL DISTRIBUTIONS

In this section we shall examine the empirical frequency distributions of three variables that appear in the dynamic equations of term structure theory. These variables are:

1. The first difference in forward rates which apply to the same future period, $r_{n,t} - r_{n+1,t-1}$ [1]
2. The first difference in yields on a *given* bill, $R_{n,t} - R_{n+1,t-1}$ [2]
3. The first difference in yields of the same maturity, $R_{n,t} - R_{n,t-1}$

In all cases, we shall use the simple arithmetic means of bid and asked rates. These distributions are of interest in their own right, for it is always worthwhile knowing whether an economic variable follows a simple probability law, and also because inferences drawn from parametric tests depend on the underlying probability functions.

A Priori Knowledge About the Distributions

Interest rate changes reflect an accumulation of new information between successive periods. This accumulation is the *sum* of many small, independent pieces of information, i.e., the sum of many individually unimportant random variables. Now the generalized central limit theorem states, if a sum of independent random variables with common distribution tends toward any limiting distribution, that distribution will be a member of the stable class (Feller, 1966, p. 168.) Thus, if interest rate changes conform to *any* probability law, they will probably conform to a stable distribution. If the empirical frequencies fit no members of the stable class, then (1) there are not many independent pieces of information arriving at the market each period,[3] or (2) the process has no limiting distribution, or (3) marked differences exist among the distributions of the individual pieces of information.

To determine whether a particular set of data fits a stable distribution well, it is necessary to estimate the characteristic exponent, α; the scale parameter, s[4]; the location parameter, δ; and the index of skewness.[5] Then one uses these estimates in a goodness-of-fit test. We proceed to do so.

Estimating the Parameters of Stable Distributions

THE SCALE PARAMETER

It is possible to standardize any stable distribution[6] by the linear operation $x = (z - \delta)/s$, where z is the nonstandardized variate, δ is the location parameter, s is the scale parameter, and x is the standardized variate. Letting x_f denote the f fractile of the distribution, this standardization formula provides

$$x_f - x_{1-f} = (z_f - z_{1-f})/s$$

or

$$s = (z_f - z_{1-f})/(x_f - x_{1-f})$$

Now, since $x_{.72} - x_{.28}$ is nearly constant and equal to 1.654 for all $\alpha \geqslant 1$ (Fama and Roll, 1968, pp. 822-824),[7] a sample estimate of s is

$$\hat{s} = (\hat{z}_{.72} - \hat{z}_{.28})/1.654 \qquad (6\text{-}1)$$

where $\hat{z}_f$ refers to the sample estimate of the f fractile.

The sample fractile estimate $\hat{z}_f$ can be obtained as follows: Let N be the sample size. The $.28(N + 1)$th *ordered* sample value is an estimate of the .28 fractile. If this is not an integer, a fractile estimate can be made by a weighted average of two adjacent order statistics. Letting k = int$[.28(N + 1)]$ be the largest integer less than $.28(N + 1)$, the weight of the kth order statistic is w_k = $(k + 1) - .28(N + 1)$ and the weight of the $(k + 1)$th order statistic is $w_{k+1} = .28(N + 1) - k$. If the distribution is symmetric, the scale parameter estimate is

$$\hat{s} = [w_{k+1}(z_{N-k} - z_{k+1}) + w_k(z_{N+1-k} - z_k)]/1.654$$

where z_j is the jth order statistic, i.e., the jth ordered sample observation.

The estimate $\hat{s}$ has a distribution which is asymptotically normal with mean s and standard deviation [when $.28(N + 1)$ is an integer] given by

$$\sigma(\hat{s}) = \frac{1}{1.654 f_{.72}} \sqrt{\frac{2(.28)(.72 - .28)}{N}}$$

(Cramer, 1946, pp. 369-370), where N is the sample size and $f_{.72}$ is the height of the density function at the .72 fractile. (For standardized stable distributions $f_{.72}$ is approximately equal to .2. Hence, for any symmetric stable distribution,

$$\sigma(\hat{s}) \doteq (1.5/N^{1/2})s$$

the exact value ranging from $(1.25/\sqrt{N})s$ for the normal to $(1.59/\sqrt{N})s$ for the Cauchy.)

THE CHARACTERISTIC EXPONENT

The range $x_{.72} - x_{.28}$ has a nearly constant value over all choices of $\alpha \geqslant 1$. No other range shares this property, and just about any other *sample* range can be used to estimate α in the following way[8]: Define

$$\hat{x}_f \equiv (\hat{z}_f - \hat{z}_{1-f})/2\hat{s}, \qquad (6\text{-}2)$$

where the $\hat{z}$'s are order statistics. Then $\hat{x}_f$ is a *consistent estimator* of the f fractile of the standardized distribution. Since this fractile is uniquely determined by α except in the special case $f = .72$, it can be used to estimate α.

Although consistent, $\hat{x}_f$ will not generally be unbiased. Furthermore, it will have an odd sampling distribution since it is the ratio of two *asymptotically* normally distributed random variables. [Marsaglia (1965) discusses the problem of ratios of normal variates.] Fortunately, for any particular choice of f, the bias[9] and sampling properties of $\hat{x}_f$ can be determined by simulation.

In the following work, we choose $f = .95$. This choice may not be optimal, but it is far from arbitrary. The range covering the middle 90 percent of the sample values has the virtue of great variation with respect to α (the larger f, the greater the corresponding range will vary over α) and a relatively small sampling variance (since the standard deviation of the range is inversely proportional to the density at the chosen fractile, the larger f, the larger will be the sampling variance of the range).

A monte carlo simulation of $\hat{x}_{.95}$ was performed for $\alpha = 1.0, 1.1, 1.3, 1.5, 1.7, 1.9,$ and 2.0 and a sample size of 299. This sample size is close to some of those used in the data analysis later. The number of replications is 101. Figure 6-1 presents the results. The bias for this sample size is trivial and the interquartile range suggests that estimates of α for sample sizes of 300 or larger are usually close to the true value.

In the following analysis, point estimates of α are obtained from the curves of Figure 6-1. The procedure is

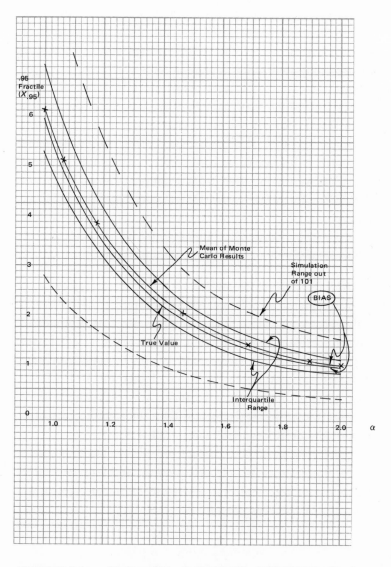

FIGURE 6-1.   .95 Fractiles of Standardized Stable Distributions
and Monte Carlo Results for $\hat{x} = .95$, $N = 299$

as follows: First, the data are ranked and $\hat{x}_{.95}$ is calculated according to equation (6-2). Second, the point estimate of α is read from one of the curves in Figure 6-1 at the level of the computed $\hat{x}_{.95}$. For sample sizes near 300, the curve labeled "mean . . ." is used since it represents expected values, including small-sample bias, based on the monte carlo results for sample sizes near 300. For sample sizes near 550 and 800, the "true value" curve is used since the estimator is known to be consistent. For example, suppose $\hat{x}_{.95} = 3.6$ were computed from a sample of size 300. From the "mean of monte carlo results" curve in Figure 6-1, we observe that $\hat{x}_{.95} = 3.6$ corresponds to an alpha of 1.36 and thus our point estimate of alpha would be $\hat{\alpha} = 1.36$.

Other methods of estimating α are possible.[10]

THE LOCATION PARAMETER

Although the sample mean is a minimum variance, linear, unbiased estimator of location when the first moment of the distribution exists (when $\alpha > 1$), when $\alpha < 2$ it is not "best" among the wider class of linear and nonlinear unbiased estimators. In particular, Fama and Roll (1968) have shown that a truncated mean always has a sampling distribution with less dispersion than the sampling distribution of the nontruncated mean, when $1 < \alpha < 2$.

The truncated mean is defined as follows: Let $z_1, z_2, \ldots,$ z_N be the *ordered* sample observations and let τ be a number between zero and one. Then the τ truncated mean for a sample of size N is given by

$$\overline{z}_{\tau,N} = \sum_{j=n_l}^{n_u} z_j/(n_u - n_l + 1)$$

where $n_l = \text{int}[N\tau/2] + 1$ and $n_u = N - \text{int}[N\tau/2]$.

Fama and Roll (1968) provide evidence that the $\tau = .5$ truncated mean has a relatively (to other truncated means) low sampling variance over a wide range of members of the symmetric stable class. Consequently, it will be used exclusively as an estimate of location in the following analysis.

Results of Distribution Fitting

Tables 6-1, 6-2, and 6-3 present estimates of s and α for the three variables under consideration. Each table has two parts. The first part is for the period October 1949 through December 1964 and contains 12 or 13 maturities. The second part is for the later period, March 1959 through December 1964, when 25 or 26 maturities were available. In addition to $\hat{\alpha}$ and $\hat{s}$, the tables contain measures of the skewness of the sampling distributions and measures of goodness of fit to the symmetric stable distribution with $\alpha = \hat{\alpha}$.

RESULTS FOR α

Estimates of the characteristic exponent are relatively uniform over all maturities in the three tables. The exception occurs in Table 6-1 at maturities greater than 12 weeks.

Values of $\hat{\alpha}$ for U.S. Treasury bill interest rate changes are lower than those found by others for different economic variables. Fama, for example, using different estimating techniques, found that common stock price changes conform to stable distributions with characteristic exponents of 1.8 or larger (1965, pp. 60-68). In contrast, the $\hat{\alpha}$'s for Tables 6-1, 6-2, and 6-3 are nearly all below 1.5 and some are even as small as 1.0.

TABLE 6-1   Distribution Statistics for $r_{n,t} - r_{n+1,t-1}$, U.S. Treasury Bill Forward Rate Changes, October 1949-December 1964, Weekly Observations

Maturity, n (weeks)	$\hat{\alpha}$	$\hat{s}$ (%/annum)	Skewness ($\% < \bar{z}_{.5,N}$)	χ^2	N
	Part 1.	*October 1949-December 1964*			
1	1.43	.102	48.8	47.0	795
2	1.44	.0925	48.6	116	795
3	1.46	.105	48.8	60.2	795
4	1.46	.114	47.9	81.6	795
5	1.30	.103	47.0	54.4	795
6	1.37	.110	48.6	34.6	795
7	1.34	.115	47.3	57.3	795
8	1.31	.110	46.3	69.0	795
9	1.25	.109	52.8	61.9	795
10	1.22	.105	53.6	56.5	795
11	1.27	.107	47.6	48.9	795
12	1.72	.249	47.2	174	769
	Part 2.	*March 1959-December 1964*			
1	1.35	.107	47.7	12.2	304
2	1.31	.0954	50.3	52.3	304
3	1.50	.107	48.7	22.0	304
4	1.42	.129	49.7	41.3	304
5	1.21	.105	48.0	31.6	304
6	1.32	.120	49.7	26.2	304
7	1.33	.121	48.7	27.1	304
8	1.31	.122	47.0	22.7	304
9	1.23	.122	52.3	13.4	304
10	1.13	.111	54.0	24.9	304
11	1.18	.110	52.0	18.9	304
12	1.30	.184	46.4	62.5	304
13	1.74	.507	52.3	88.9	304
14	1.40	.295	48.4	61.9	304
15	1.16	.180	43.1	55.1	304
16	1.08	.122	45.7	52.5	304
17	1.00	.119	50.3	33.4	304
18	1.25	.151	44.4	76.7	304
19	1.00	.127	52.0	40.3	304
20	1.02	.132	46.4	85.2	304
21	1.00	.122	48.0	49.4	304
22	1.00	.146	50.3	51.6	304
23	1.16	.169	47.0	58.0	304
24	1.21	.215	44.7	57.1	304
25	1.29	.287	46.7	20.7	291

TABLE 6-2   Distribution Statistics for $R_{n,t} - R_{n+1,t-1}$, U.S. Treasury Bill Yield Changes, October 1949-December 1964, Weekly Observations

Maturity, n (weeks)	$\hat{\alpha}$	$\hat{s}$ (%/annum)	Skewness (% $<\bar{z}_{.5,N}$)	χ^2	N
	Part 1.	October 1949-December 1964			
1	1.53	.0977	48.4	33.6	795
2	1.44	.0829	49.2	103	795
3	1.46	.0765	47.2	73.9	795
4	1.48	.0738	46.0	73.9	795
5	1.42	.0644	45.5	118	795
6	1.38	.0611	50.1	96.0	795
7	1.43	.0581	47.6	102	795
8	1.34	.0493	47.0	103	795
9	1.42	.0526	46.3	118	795
10	1.31	.0460	46.9	57.4	795
11	1.28	.0432	47.9	51.0	795
12	1.31	.0472	47.1	119	769
	Part 2.	March 1959-December 1964			
1	1.32	.0798	50.0	35.1	304
2	1.37	.0783	51.6	31.1	304
3	1.44	.0732	50.3	30.0	304
4	1.28	.0631	49.7	37.8	304
5	1.37	.0600	46.4	69.6	304
6	1.31	.0549	48.0	48.4	304
7	1.26	.0490	47.4	44.2	304
8	1.23	.0429	46.7	53.0	304
9	1.20	.0388	47.0	33.7	304
10	1.17	.0369	49.7	41.7	304
11	1.13	.0366	49.0	36.7	304
12	1.13	.0398	49.3	27.6	304
13	1.18	.0462	53.6	47.2	304
14	1.19	.0429	49.7	45.7	304
15	1.22	.0371	48.4	61.4	304
16	1.24	.0366	46.7	46.9	304
17	1.21	.0358	47.0	80.4	304
18	1.14	.0308	50.3	76.9	304
19	1.17	.0308	50.0	60.1	304
20	1.17	.0325	47.7	57.2	304
21	1.15	.0308	46.1	53.8	304
22	1.15	.0340	51.3	46.3	304
23	1.22	.0366	50.3	29.9	304
24	1.20	.0385	50.0	13.3	304
25	1.19	.0397	50.9	21.7	291

TABLE 6-3   Distribution Statistics for $R_{n,t} - R_{n,t-1}$, U.S. Treasury Bill Yield Changes, October 1949-December 1964, Weekly Observations

Maturity, n (weeks)	$\hat{\alpha}$	$\hat{s}$ (%/annum)	Skewness (%$<\bar{z}_{.5,N}$)	χ^2	N
		Part 1.	*October 1949-December 1964*		
1	1.40	.0953	46.0	77.4	795
2	1.41	.0922	47.7	86.0	795
3	1.60	.0949	53.2	52.8	795
4	1.49	.0862	52.6	72.4	795
5	1.41	.0735	52.8	66.4	795
6	1.35	.0644	50.9	68.0	795
7	1.35	.0584	52.0	88.8	795
8	1.29	.0526	51.2	91.5	795
9	1.34	.0550	52.2	74.4	795
10	1.31	.0490	50.2	71.4	795
11	1.26	.0432	51.1	48.6	795
12	1.29	.0466	49.9	52.3	795
13	1.35	.0516	50.7	46.9	746
		Part 2.	*March 1959-December 1964*		
1	1.27	.0921	48.7	21.5	304
2	1.28	.0848	49.3	37.6	304
3	1.50	.0888	46.7	31.0	304
4	1.44	.0857	50.7	36.2	304
5	1.27	.0617	46.4	40.2	304
6	1.31	.0614	52.0	44.3	304
7	1.32	.0549	52.0	24.2	304
8	1.12	.0428	49.3	23.1	304
9	1.25	.0446	50.0	33.5	304
10	1.20	.0429	51.6	35.5	304
11	1.20	.0398	49.3	24.9	304
12	1.12	.0398	49.7	19.0	304
13	1.33	.0429	51.3	22.7	304
14	1.17	.0431	51.3	20.3	304
15	1.34	.0461	54.3	39.6	304
16	1.35	.0427	51.3	27.7	304
17	1.37	.0426	54.3	47.7	304
18	1.26	.0398	49.7	34.5	304
19	1.36	.0429	52.6	35.1	304
20	1.21	.0355	51.0	34.1	304
21	1.25	.0368	53.6	23.6	304
22	1.13	.0311	51.6	41.4	304
23	1.12	.0337	51.0	41.7	304
24	1.18	.0358	50.7	36.5	304
25	1.20	.0426	51.6	12.3	304
26	1.16	.0428	52.3	28.8	279

Rough estimates of the confidence level on $\hat{\alpha}$ can be obtained from Figure 6-1. As an example, let us select maturity 11, Table 6-3, part 2, which has $\hat{\alpha} = 1.20$ and a sample size of 304. Recall that the estimate $\hat{\alpha} = 1.20$ was taken from the "mean . . ." curve of Figure 6-1. We can thus tell that $\hat{x}_{.95}$ was about 4.48. The two interquartile range curves pass through the level $\hat{x}_{.95} = 4.48$ at about the points $\alpha = 1.15$ and $\alpha = 1.26$. Consequently, in about half the cases, repeated samples of this size from a symmetric stable distribution with $\alpha = 1.20$ will result in estimates of α between 1.15 and 1.26.[11]

With a large degree of confidence, most of the distributions of interest rate changes have α significantly lower than 2 and are thus nonnormal. Indeed, the upper limit of the simulation range suggests that most of the α's are significantly lower than 1.5.

RESULTS FOR S

Except for maturities near 13 weeks, the estimates of scale follow regular patterns.

The scale parameter estimates for the two yield changes, $R_{n,t} - R_{n,t-1}$ of Table 6-3 and $R_{n,t} - R_{n+1,t-1}$ of Table 6-2, decline substantially with maturity. In contrast, forward rate changes (Table 6-1) have scale parameters that increase with maturity. This pattern is no doubt due to the definition of forward rates. Recall that

$$r_{n,t} = nR_{n,t} - (n - 1)R_{n-1,t} .$$

If $R_{n,t}$ and $R_{n-1,t}$ happened to be normally and independently distributed,

$$\text{var}(\widetilde{r}_{n,t}) = n^2 \, \text{var}(\widetilde{R}_{n,t}) + (n - 1)^2 \, \text{var}(\widetilde{R}_{n-1,t})$$

and the scale parameter (the standard deviation) of $r_{n,t}$ would be on the order of $(\sqrt{2})n$ times as large as the scale parameter of the yields. A similar addition rule holds for the scale parameter of other stable distributions [cf. equation (6-8)]. If $R_{n,t}$ and $R_{n-1,t}$ are less than perfectly correlated, the scale parameter of the forward rate will increase substantially with maturity. (The scale parameters of the yields *could*, of course, decline enough with maturity to offset this effect, but such is evidently not the case in the present instance.)

SKEWNESS

Skewness is measured by the percentage of sample observations less than the .5 truncated mean,[12] $\overline{z}_{.5,N}$. If the underlying process is symmetric, this value should be 50 percent. Under the null hypothesis that the distribution is symmetric, the probability of an observation below the mean is .5; and with sample sizes this large, the statistic

$$\frac{\left(\dfrac{\% \text{ below mean}}{100} - \dfrac{1}{2}\right)\sqrt{N}}{\dfrac{1}{2}}$$

has a normal distribution with mean zero and variance one.

If the null hypothesis were true and the sample size N were 795 (as it is in parts 1 of the tables), the 95 percent acceptance interval on the percentage of observations below the mean is $46.3 - 53.7$. If we decide to reject the null hypothesis if the observed percentage is outside this interval, in only 3 of the 37 cases in parts 1 of the three tables would the null hypothesis be rejected.

For smaller sample sizes, the 95 percent acceptance interval is larger. For $N = 304$, the interval is $44.9 - 55.1$. In only 3 of the 73 cases in parts 2 of the tables (where the sample size is 304) would the null hypothesis be rejected. Conclusion: At this significance level, there is no evidence of asymmetry in the empirical distributions.

THE GOODNESS-OF-FIT RESULTS

The goodness-of-fit test results are somewhat less favorable to the hypothesis that the distributions are symmetric stable. For this test, the sample values were sorted and standardized by subtracting the .5 truncated mean and dividing by $\hat{s}$. Then the number of observations falling in each of the 22 intervals indicated in Table 6-4 was determined. (The table shows only the 11 intervals above zero. The intervals below zero are exactly the same but with opposite signs.) Also included in Table 6-4, as an example, is the probability that a standardized symmetric stable variable with $\hat{\alpha} = 1.2$ will fall in the interval.

TABLE 6-4   Intervals Used for
Goodness-of-Fit Tests

Interval, i	Probability ($\alpha = 1.2$)
0-.25	.0740
.25-.50	.0690
.50-.75	.0603
.75-1.00	.0503
1.00-1.50	.0728
1.50-2.00	.0456
2.00-2.50	.0292
2.50-3.00	.0195
3.00-3.50	.0137
3.50-4.00	.0100
Greater than 4.00	.0558

The variable

$$\sum_{i=1}^{22} \frac{(\nu_i - P_{i,\hat{\alpha}} N)^2}{P_{i,\hat{\alpha}} N}$$

(where N is the total sample size, ν_i is the number of observations falling in interval i, and $P_{i,\hat{\alpha}}$ is the probability that a standardized symmetric stable variable with $\alpha = \hat{\alpha}$ will fall in interval i) is approximately distributed as χ^2 with 18 degrees of freedom[13] under the null hypothesis that the distribution is symmetric stable with $s = \hat{s}$, $\alpha = \hat{\alpha}$, and location parameter $\delta = \overline{z}_{.5,N}$. This χ^2 distribution has a mean of 18 and the .99 fractile is 34.8. Most of the χ^2 values in the tables exceed 34.8! It would appear that either we have misestimated α or s or else the distributions are not members of the symmetric stable class.

To isolate the reason for this poor fit, we have performed some sensitivity analyses to determine how the χ^2 value changes with $\hat{\alpha}$. Two of these results are presented in Table 6-5, one with a low χ^2, maturity 23 of part 2 of Table 6-2, and one with a high χ^2, maturity 17 of the same table, part 2.

These results are typical of those generally obtained. *Although the χ^2 value is high, it is a minimum very close to the point estimate $\hat{\alpha}$* (which is starred in Table 6-5). Thus, the stable distribution with $\alpha = \hat{\alpha}$ does not seem to fit very well, but it fits better than any other symmetric stable distribution.

Since a poor estimate of α does not seem to be responsible for the large χ^2 values, we are motivated to look further for the cause by plotting histograms of the empirical distributions. One such distribution (for $n = 17$ from

TABLE 6-5 Selected Sensitivity Analyses for x^2
Relative to $\hat{\alpha}, R_{n,t} - R_{n+1,t-1}$
March 1959-December 1964

$n = 17$		$n = 23$	
$\hat{\alpha}$	x^2	$\hat{\alpha}$	x^2
1.07	83.102	1.08	31.570
1.09	82.275	1.10	30.992
1.11	81.625	1.12	30.545
1.13	81.101	1.14	30.204
1.15	80.721	1.16	29.966
1.17	80.466	1.18	29.846
1.19	80.302	1.20	29.815
1.21*	80.422	1.22*	29.913
1.23	80.450	1.24	30.108
1.25	80.823	1.26	30.413
1.27	81.219	1.28	30.829
1.29	81.748	1.30	31.367
1.31	82.452	1.32	32.010
1.33	83.290	1.34	32.770
1.35	84.255	1.36	33.622

Table 6-2, part 2, or the example on the left in Table 6-5) is plotted in Figure 6-2. The heavy lines represent the stable distribution for $\alpha = 1.21$. ($\hat{\alpha} = 1.21$ was estimated for these data.) The dotted lines depict the empirical frequency distribution. Both the true scale, for changes in yields in units of percent per annum, and the standardized scale are shown. The mean yield change is $-.0113$ percent per annum.

For the distribution shown in Figure 6-2, the largest contribution to χ^2 obviously comes from the enormous differences between the expected and observed counts near the mean. These differences are largely due to discontinuities in yield quotations. Yields can change only in increments of one-half or one basis point (.01 percent) since the quote cards report the yields to only two places past the decimal point. If either the bid yield or the asked

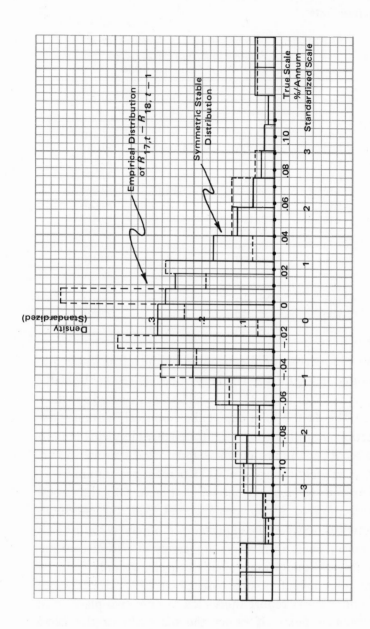

FIGURE 6-2. Distribution of $R_{17,t} - R_{18,t-1}$ and Distribution of Symmetric Stable Variable, $\alpha = 1.21, s = 1.0$

TABLE 6-6   Distribution of $R_{17,t} - R_{18,t-1}$ Near Its Mean

Yield Change (% per annum)	Number of Observations at this Change	Count in χ^2 Interval	Expected Count
−.025	5	30	20.9
−.020	25		
−.015	3	3	22.4
	$\hat{\bar{x}} = -.0113$		
−.010	14	17	22.4
−.005	3		
0	34	41	20.9
.005	7		
.010	13	13	18.3
.015	5	21	15.3
.020	16		

yield, but not both, changes by .01 percent, the total
change of the bid-asked average is, of course, .005 percent.

Table 6-6 presents the complete distribution of the yield
changes of Figure 6-2 for the interval

$$-.03 < R_{17,t} - R_{18,t-1} < .03$$

(The intervals used for calculation of χ^2 are separated by
horizontal lines.) From this table, it is quite clear that both
the bid and asked yields usually change by the same number of basis points because the one-half basis point values
−.025, −.015, −.005, etc., have much lower counts than
the even basis point values −.020, −.010, etc.

It is also clear that small changes in the mean or a
choice of slightly different intervals could cause an enormous difference in the χ^2 value. For example, if only four

TABLE 6-7   Distribution of $R_{23,t} - R_{24,t-1}$ Near Its Mean

Yield Change (% per annum)	Number of Observations at this Change	Count in χ^2 Interval	Expected Count
−.025	6	27	20.9
−.020	21		
−.015	3	25	22.3
−.010	22		
$\hat{x} = -.008$			
−.005	8	30	22.3
0	22		
.005	9	24	20.9
.010	15		
.015	4	4	18.3
.020	17	21	15.3
.025	4		

intervals were chosen between plus and minus $1\hat{s}$ rather than eight intervals, the χ^2 value would fall from 80.4 to 39.2! This is further emphasized by the distribution of $R_{23,t} - R_{24,t-1}$ (the companion example to $R_{17,t} - R_{18,t-1}$ in Table 6-5) near its mean. This distribution is given in Table 6-7.

A very similar pattern to that of Table 6-6 is evident; but in Table 6-7, the mean and $\hat{s}$ just happen to fall such that the intervals obtained produce a low value of χ^2.

In conclusion, the discreteness of the data destroys the ability of the χ^2 goodness-of-fit test. This discreteness should not, however, affect statistical methods which do not require the data to be split into classes, and in these cases the evidence is strong that the theory of symmetric stable distributions can be useful. This evidence consists of

(1) the generalized central limit theorem; (2) empirical measures of skewness which show that the empirical distributions are symmetric; (3) empirical evidence that although χ^2 values are high due to discrete data, they are minimized by the particular member of the stable family chosen (i.e., by the empirically determined values of $\hat\alpha$ and $\hat s$).

Symmetric stable distributions are evidently better models of the data distributions than are any other *continuous* distributions and are probably more useful than any discrete model. The cost of introducing discrete (and more complex) distributional models such as Markov models probably outweighs the benefits in changed inferences one can reasonably expect to obtain. Consequently, we shall henceforth use the theory of stable probability laws for statistical inference.

HOW TO TEST STABLE VARIABLES FOR MARTINGALE BEHAVIOR

We consider two cases: the submartingale sequences

$$E_{t-1}(\widetilde{Z}_t) = a'_t Z_{t-1}$$

$$E_{t-1}(\widetilde{Y}_t) = a_t + Y_{t-1} \tag{6-3}$$

where a_t and a'_t are known constants, the expectations operator E_{t-1} is understood to be conditional on the state of information in period $t-1$, and $\widetilde{Z}$ and $\widetilde{Y}$ are random variables. The following discussion will concentrate on the additive form of (6-3), but whatever is discovered for the first difference, $\widetilde{X}_t = \widetilde{Y}_t - \widetilde{Y}_{t-1}$ applies equally to the relative $\widetilde{Z}_t/\widetilde{Z}_{t-1}$, in case the submartingale is of the multiplicative form. (For a pure martingale, $a_t = 0$ or $a'_t = 1$ for all t.)

Properties of Submartingales Useful for Testing

THE EXPECTED FIRST DIFFERENCE

Equation (6-3) can be written in terms of the first difference $\widetilde{X}_t = \widetilde{Y}_t - \widetilde{Y}_{t-1}$ as $E_{t-1}(\widetilde{X}_t \mid Y_{t-1}) = a_t$. This is possible because in $t - 1$, when the expectation is conditioned, Y_{t-1} has already been observed and is therefore non-stochastic. But if $E_{t-1}(\widetilde{X}_t \mid Y_{t-1}) = a_t$ and if $a_t = a$ is constant over all t, the conditioning variable is irrelevant and

$$E_{t-1}(\widetilde{X}_t \mid Y_{t-1}) = E(\widetilde{X}_t) = a \qquad (6\text{-}4)$$

COVARIANCE OF MARTINGALE RELATIVES

For submartingales of the additive form of (6-3), the first differences are linearly independent. This means that the serial covariance is zero over all nonzero lags. *Proof*: Assume that X_t and X_{t-1} have integrable density functions $p(X_t)$ and $p(X_{t-1})$ and an integrable joint density function $p(X_t, X_{t-1})$ and that all the following integrals converge. The covariance is defined as

$$\text{cov}(\widetilde{X}_t, \widetilde{X}_{t-1}) = \int_{X_t} \int_{X_{t-1}} [X_t - E(\widetilde{X}_t)] \, [X_{t-1} - E(\widetilde{X}_{t-1})]$$

$$p(X_t, X_{t-1}) \, dX_{t-1} \, dX_t$$

$$= \int_{X_{t-1}} [X_{t-1} - E(\widetilde{X}_{t-1})] \int_{X_t} [X_t - E(\widetilde{X}_t)]$$

$$p(X_t \mid X_{t-1}) \, dX_t \; p(X_{t-1}) \, dX_{t-1}$$

$$= \int_{X_{t-1}} [E(\widetilde{X}_t \mid X_{t-1}) - E(\widetilde{X}_t)] \, [X_{t-1} - E(\widetilde{X}_{t-1})]$$

$$p(X_{t-1}) \, dX_{t-1} \,^{14} \qquad (6\text{-}5)$$

but we have already seen[15] that $E(\widetilde{X}_t \mid X_{t-1}) = E(\widetilde{X}_t) = a_{x}$. Consequently, the first term in brackets and the covariance are identically zero. The proof obviously applies to any covariance, $\text{cov}(\widetilde{X}_t, \widetilde{X}_{t+j})$, where $j \neq 0$. Note that X_t and X_{t-1} have not been assumed independent.[16] This would have required $p(X_t \mid X_{t-1}) = p(X_t)$.

Parametric Tests of Martingale Behavior

If the variable $\widetilde{Y}$ follows a submartingale sequence of the form $E_{t-1}(Y_t) = a_t + Y_{t-1}$, we have seen that

1. If $a_t = a$, $E_{t-1}(\widetilde{Y}_t - Y_{t-1}) = E(\widetilde{Y}_t - Y_{t-1}) = a$.
2. $\text{cov}(\widetilde{Y}_t - \widetilde{Y}_{t-1}, \widetilde{Y}_{t-1} - \widetilde{Y}_{t-2}) = 0$.

Thus, two obvious parametric tests of the martingale property are (1) the means test, testing the deviation of the .5 truncated sample mean from a, and (2) the covariance test, testing the deviation of the sample covariance from zero. Both the truncated mean and the sample covariance are unbiased estimates of their population counterparts[17] and the tests can be implemented as soon as measures of dispersion are developed.

THE MEANS TEST

This section will derive the asymptotic standard deviation of the .5 truncated sample mean. Recall that $z_1, z_2, \ldots, z_N$ are the ordered sample observations and that the .5 truncated mean is given by

$$\bar{z}_{.5,N} = \sum_{j=n_l}^{n_u} z_j/(n_u - n_l + 1)$$

where $n_l = \text{int}(N/4) + 1$ and $n_u = N - \text{int}(N/4)$, and where N is the sample size.

We have already mentioned (see p. 65) that the distribution of z_j is asymptotically normal with mean $p_j = j/(N + 1)$ and variance

$$\frac{p_j(1 - p_j)}{N f_j^2}$$

where f_j is the density at the $j/(N + 1)$ fractile of the underlying probability distribution (which generated the z's). The asymptotic covariance of any two-order statistics, $z_j < z_k$, is

$$\frac{p_j(1 - p_k)}{N f_j f_k}$$

See Kendall and Stuart (1963, Chapter XIV).

Consequently, the asymptotic variance of $\widetilde{\overline{z}}_{.5,N}$ is

$$\text{var}(\widetilde{\overline{z}}_{.5,N}) = \left(\frac{1}{n_u - n_l + 1}\right)^2 \left[\sum_{j=n_l}^{n_u} \frac{p_j(1 - p_j)}{N f_j^2} + 2 \sum_{j=n_l}^{n_u-1} \sum_{k=j+1}^{n_u} \frac{p_j(1 - p_k)}{N f_j f_k}\right]$$

If we denote the density of a standardized $(s = 1)$ distribution by ϕ_j, then the density of any other distribution with the same characteristic exponent, α, is $f_j = \phi_j/s$. Thus, we have for the asymptotic standard deviation of the truncated mean

$$\sigma(\widetilde{\overline{z}}_{.5,N}) = s\sigma(\widetilde{\overline{x}}_{.5,N})$$

where $\widetilde{\overline{x}}_{.5,N}$ is the .5 truncated mean for a sample of size N from a *standardized* distribution with the same α.

Some values of $\sigma(\widetilde{\overline{x}}_{.5,N})$ for the standardized Cauchy ($\alpha = 1$) and normal ($\alpha = 2$) distributions are given in Table 6-8. This table shows that Cauchy and normal values of $\sigma(\widetilde{\overline{x}}_{.5,N})$ are almost equal at each sample size (a fact true for the .5 and nearby truncated means but for no others). The standard deviations of .5 truncated means for other stable distribution, $1 < \alpha < 2$, lie between the values in Table 6-8. Therefore, a precise estimate of the standard deviation of the .5 truncated sample mean is given by

$$\sigma(\widetilde{\overline{z}}_{.5,N}) = [(2 - \hat{\alpha})\sigma_{C,N}(\widetilde{\overline{x}}_{.5,N}) + (\hat{\alpha} - 1)\sigma_{\eta,N}(\widetilde{\overline{x}}_{.5,N})]\,\hat{s} \qquad (6\text{-}6)$$

where $\sigma_{C,N}(\widetilde{\overline{x}}_{.5,N})$ and $\sigma_{\eta,N}(\widetilde{\overline{x}}_{.5,N})$ are the standard deviations of the .5 truncated means for standardized Cauchy and normal distributions, respectively, and $\hat{\alpha}$ and $\hat{s}$ are the sample estimates of the characteristic exponent and scale parameter for the distribution which generated the z's.

TABLE 6-8   Asymptotic Standard Deviations of .5 Truncated Means from Standard Cauchy and Normal Distributions

N (sample size)	Cauchy	Normal	Percent Deviation[a] $\left[\left(\dfrac{\text{Cauchy} - \text{Normal}}{\text{Cauchy}}\right)100\right]$
20	.353	.348	1.39
52	.220	.215	2.50
100	.159	.155	2.76
220	.108	.104	2.98
300	.0921	.0893	3.04
540	.0686	.0666	2.92
800	.0564	.0547	3.01

[a]May appear to contain errors since numbers in the second and third columns have been rounded.

The maximum bias in $\sigma(\widetilde{z}_{.5,N})$ is about 3 percent. This could occur for sample sizes above 100 if α is completely misestimated, i.e., if $\hat{\alpha} = 2$ when $\alpha = 1$ or vice versa.

THE COVARIANCE TEST[18]

The sample covariance between two variables $\widetilde{U}$ and $\widetilde{V}$ is

$$C_{U_t V_t} = \left(\frac{1}{N}\right)\sum_{t=1}^{N} (U_t - \overline{U})(V_t - \overline{V}) \qquad (6\text{-}7)$$

where $\overline{U}$ and $\overline{V}$ are estimates of the location parameters[19] of the distributions of $\widetilde{U}$ and $\widetilde{V}$ and U_t and V_t are joint observations.

Our objective is to determine the distribution and scale parameter of $C_{U_t V_t}$ conditional on the observed vector, $\mathbf{U}$, of observations on $\widetilde{U}$. Conditional on $\mathbf{U}$, $C_{U_t V_t}$ is a weighted sum of the observed vector $\mathbf{V}$ of observations on $\widetilde{V}$. Hence, if the elements of $\mathbf{V}$ are independent and identically distributed according to a stable probability law, $(C_{U_t V_t} \mid \mathbf{U})$ has a stable distribution with the same characteristic exponent as $\widetilde{V}$. This is due to the very definition of stable distributions, invariance under addition [or invariance under convolutions according to Feller (1966, pp. 50-51)].

Before deriving the scale parameter for the sample covariance, it will be necessary to state the general addition rule for scale parameters of stable variables. Each stable distribution has a parameter γ related to s by $s^{\alpha} = \gamma$. (In the normal case, $\alpha = 2$ and γ is one-half the variance.) Using this measure, the addition rule for the scale parameter of a weighted sum of independent stable random variables, $\widetilde{W}_1, \widetilde{W}_2, \ldots, \widetilde{W}_N$ with the same value of α and weights b_1, $b_2, \ldots, b_N$ is given by

$$\gamma(b_1\widetilde{W}_1 + b_2\widetilde{W}_2 + \cdots + b_N\widetilde{W}_N) = |b_1|^{\alpha}\gamma(\widetilde{W}_1)$$

$$+ |b_2|^{\alpha}\gamma(\widetilde{W}_2) + \cdots + |b_N|^{\alpha}\gamma(\widetilde{W}_N) \qquad (6\text{-}8)$$

If the $\widetilde{W}$'s are normal, equation (6-8) states the addition rule for variances. If $b_1 = b_2 = \cdots = b_N = 1/N$, (6-8) provides the scale parameter of the sample mean, i.e.,

$$\gamma(\overline{W}) = (1/N)^{\alpha}[\gamma(\widetilde{W}_1) + \cdots + \gamma(\widetilde{W}_N)]$$

and in the particular case where $\gamma(\widetilde{W}) = \gamma(\widetilde{W}_1) = \ldots = \gamma(\widetilde{W}_N)$, we have $\gamma(\overline{W}) = \gamma(\widetilde{W})(1/N)^{\alpha-1}$ or $s(\overline{W}) = s(\widetilde{W})$ $(1/N)^{1-1/\alpha}$. Again using the normal case as an example, we see that this is the formula for the standard deviation of the sample mean, $\sigma(\overline{W}) = \sigma(\widetilde{W})/\sqrt{N}$. In the Cauchy case, $\alpha = 1$, and we have $s(\overline{W}) = s(\widetilde{W})$, which is a well-known property of the Cauchy distribution that the sample mean of Cauchy variates has the same scale parameter as an individual variate.

Returning now to the sample covariance $C_{U_t V_t}$ and writing deviations about the mean in lowercase, (i.e., $v_t = V_t - \overline{V}$), equation (6-7) is

$$C_{U_t V_t} = \left(\frac{1}{N}\right)\sum_{t=1}^{N} v_t u_t$$

and the scale parameter of the conditional covariance is

$$\gamma(C_{U_t V_t} \mid \mathbf{U}) = \gamma(\widetilde{v})\sum_{t=1}^{N}\left|\frac{u_t}{N}\right|^{\alpha}$$

or

$$s(C_{U_t V_t} \mid U) = s(\widetilde{v})\left(\sum_{t=1}^{N} \mid \frac{u_t}{N} \mid^{\alpha}\right)^{1/\alpha} \qquad (6\text{-}9)$$

As a practical matter, it is appropriate to estimate $s(\widetilde{v})$ by the .72-.28 range method previously described [we designate the result $\hat{s}(\widetilde{v})$] and to estimate α by the ratio of ranges method, the result being denoted $\hat{\alpha}$. Using these quantities, the point estimate of the scale parameter of the covariance is

$$\hat{s}(C_{U_t V_t} \mid U) = [\hat{s}(\widetilde{v})/N]\left(\sum_{t=1}^{N} \mid u_t \mid^{\hat{\alpha}}\right)^{1/\hat{\alpha}} \qquad (6\text{-}10)$$

For simplicity of notation, we shall hereafter denote $(C_{U_t V_t} \mid U)$ by C when the identities of **U** and **V** are clear.

Nonparametric Tests of Covariance

If the population covariance cov $(\widetilde{U}, \widetilde{V})$ is zero, the sample covariance is unbiased and has a symmetric distribution.[20] Consequently, inferences about the deviation of the population covariance from zero can be accomplished by nonparametric methods. The experimental design is:

1. Split the data into subsamples (i.e., subperiods of the time series).
2. Calculate $C_{U_t V_t}$ for each subperiod.
3. Assume the subperiods are independent.
4. Calculate the binomial probabilities for the signs of $C_{U_t V_t}$, the hypothesis being that positive and negative signs are equally likely.[21]

EMPIRICAL TESTS OF TERM STRUCTURE THEORIES

The dynamic equations for yields and forward rates under the several term structure hypotheses were derived in Chapter 4. For reference, these results are tabulated in Table 6-9. We now restate several definitions:

1. $r_{j,t}$ is the one-period forward rate, observed in period t, which is supposed to prevail at the beginning of period $t + j - 1$.
2. $R_{j,t}$ is the j-period yield as of period t.
3. The liquidity premium $L_{j,t} = r_{j,t} - E_t(\widetilde{R}_{1,t+j-1})$, where $E_t(\widetilde{R}_{1,t+j-1})$ is the market expectation, conditional on all information as of period t, of the future one-period spot rate to begin at $t + j - 1$. (Since $r_{1,t} = R_{1,t}$, obviously $L_{1,t} = 0$.)

4. a_j and $A_n = \sum_{j=1}^{n} a_j$ are constants.

The nine equations in the top three rows of Table 6-9 involve the forward rate first difference $r_{j,t} - r_{j+1,t-1}$ and the two yield first differences $R_{j,t} - R_{j+1,t-1}$ and $R_{j,t} - R_{j,t-1}$. We have already determined that these variables have symmetric stable distributions. We shall now calculate their expected values and determine whether they are serially correlated or serially dependent.

At the same time, the three term structure theories will be subjected to a discriminatory test, for we shall argue that each hypothesis implies that a different one of the three variables is serially uncorrelated.

TABLE 6-9 Dynamic Yield and Forward Rate Equations Implied by the Term Structure Hypotheses

Variable	Hypothesis		
	Pure Expectations (1)	Time-Dependent Market Segmentation (2)	Stationary Market Segmentation or Liquidity Preference (3)
$E_{t-1}(\tilde{r}_{j,t} - r_{j+1,t-1}) =$	0	$R_{j,t-1} - R_{j+1,t-1} + a_j$	$L_{j,t-1} - L_{j+1,t-1}$
$E_{t-1}(\tilde{R}_{j,t} - R_{j+1,t-1}) =$	$\frac{1}{j}(R_{j+1,t-1} - R_{1,t-1})$	A_j	$\frac{1}{j}(B_{j+1,t-1} - R_{1,t-1} - L_{j+1,t-1})$
$E_{t-1}(\tilde{R}_{j,t} - R_{j,t-1}) =$	$\frac{1}{j}(r_{j+1,t-1} - r_{1,t-1})$	$R_{j+1,t-1} - R_{j,t-1} + A_j$	$\frac{1}{j}(r_{j+1,t-1} - R_{1,t-1} - L_{j+1,t-1})$
$E_{t-1}\left[\log_e\left(\dfrac{\tilde{p}_{j,t}}{p_{j+1,t-1}}\right)\right] =$	$R_{1,t-1}$	$R_{j+1,t-1} - jA_j$	$R_{1,t-1} + L_{j+1,t-1}$

The last row contains the expected log price relative under each hypothesis.

The Pure Expectations Hypothesis

THE TESTABLE EQUATION

From Table 6-9 the serially uncorrelated variable under this hypothesis is quite obvious. The forward rate sequence $(r_{j,t}, r_{j-1,t+1}, \ldots)$ is a pure martingale, since the hypothesis states[22] that $E_{t-1}(\tilde{r}_{j,t} - r_{j+1,t-1}) = 0$. If the hypothesis is valid, the sample mean forward rate first difference and the sample covariance

$$C_{r_{j,t}-r_{j+1,t-1}, r_{j+1,t-1}-r_{j+2,t-2}}$$

must be insignificantly different from zero.[23]

THE EMPIRICAL EVIDENCE

Table 6-10 presents three statistics which test these propositions. First, the "mean" in column 2 is the .5 truncated sample mean. Under the null hypothesis (in this case the pure expectations hypothesis) the .5 truncated sample mean has a normal distribution with mean zero and standard deviation computed according to (6-6). Second, the C in column 4 is the sample covariance given by (6-7). Conditional on the observed values of the "independent" variable, this statistic has a stable distribution with $\alpha = \hat{\alpha}$. (The estimates of α are given in Table 6-1. The scale parameter for the sample covariance was derived on p. 87.) Third, Table 6-10 contains two-way contingency table tests of the serial dependence in forward rate changes.[24] These results are given in column 6, labeled χ^2. The contingency table was divided into four cells based on the following paired occurrences:

TABLE 6-10   Tests of the Pure Expectations Hypothesis with
Sample Means and Serial Covariances of U.S.
Treasury Bill Forward Rate Changes, Weekly
Observations, October 1949-December 1964

Maturity (weeks)	Mean (%/annum) $\times 10^2$	$\dfrac{\|\text{Mean}\|}{\text{Standard Error}}$	C (%/annum)^2 $\times 10^3$	$\dfrac{\|C\|}{\hat{s}(C)}$	χ^2	N
Part 1. October 1949-December 1964						
1	−1.59*	2.80	−.788	.365	.0464	794
2	−4.06*	7.89	2.99	1.41	.0114	794
3	−7.23*	12.4	6.80	2.78	.630	794
4	−7.93*	12.5	−4.04	1.48	6.32*	794
5	−3.14*	5.45	−8.21	1.98	10.6*	794
6	−1.36	2.22	−13.3	3.63	8.87*	794
7	−2.05*	3.19	−10.3	2.37	16.6*	794
8	−2.98*	4.84	−25.0	5.19	28.3*	794
9	0.462	.757	−19.3	3.26	18.8*	794
10	2.61*	4.44	−7.20	1.16	5.43*	794
11	−2.70	4.51	−2.68	3.12	17.4*	794
Part 2. March 1959-December 1964						
1	−0.704	.722	−1.33	.327	.686	303
2	−4.85*	5.57	5.75	1.30	.0600	303
3	−11.2*	11.5	9.15	2.71	3.35	303
4	−12.3*	10.5	−6.47	1.28	.798	303
5	−3.20*	3.33	−8.41	1.03	5.39*	303
6	−2.45*	2.24	−19.5	2.93	.267	303
7	−3.63*	3.29	−19.3	2.76	14.7*	303
8	−6.15*	5.53	−28.2	3.87	5.16*	303
9	1.83	1.64	−24.1	2.57	7.13*	303
10	3.08*	3.02	−19.0	1.65	6.42*	303
11	−1.86	1.85	−28.4	1.96	11.0*	303
12	−14.8*	8.81	−211	6.05	16.1*	303
13	52.2*	11.4	−427*	15.7	38.0*	303
14	−29.3*	10.9	−63.1	2.73	5.44*	303
15	−7.26*	4.40	−74.2	2.93	4.67*	303
16	−3.29*	2.94	−15.5	.678	8.59*	303
17	−1.34	1.22	−26.4	.814	5.34*	303
18	−6.75*	4.89	−54.8	3.21	9.23*	303
19	−.548	.469	−14.4	.336	.120	303
20	−3.47*	2.86	−131	3.30	11.1*	303
21	−.922	.821	−162	3.57	1.94	303
22	−.491	.365	−140	3.14	1.91	303
23	−1.78	1.15	−3.62	.121	.567	303
24	−3.67	1.87	−112	2.69	9.77*	290

1. $r_{j,t} - r_{j+1,t-1} < 0$ and $r_{j+1,t-1} - r_{j+2,t-2} < 0$.
2. $r_{j,t} - r_{j+1,t-1} < 0$ and $r_{j+1,t-1} - r_{j+2,t-2} > 0$.
3. $r_{j,t} - r_{j+1,t-1} > 0$ and $r_{j+1,t-1} - r_{j+2,t-2} < 0$.
4. $r_{j,t} - r_{j+1,t-1} > 0$ and $r_{j+1,t-1} - r_{j+2,t-2} > 0$.

Table 6-10 is broken into two parts like Tables 6-1, 6-2, and 6-3 on distribution statistics. The first part is for the period October 1949-December 1964, and the second covers the period March 1959-December 1964.

Values in the table are starred if they reject the null hypothesis that the mean or covariance is zero at a 95 percent level of confidence. The criterion is based on a two-tailed test. Thus, if the .5 truncated sample mean is outside the interval $\pm 1.96\sigma(\widetilde{z}_{.5,N})$, it is starred. Since the .5 truncated mean is asymptotically normal with mean zero under the null hypothesis, the probability that it falls within the interval is .95.

Sample covariances[25] are starred if they fall outside the 95 percent confidence interval of the appropriate stable distribution. For example, the value of $C/\hat{s}(C)$ for maturity 12 of part 2 of the table is -6.05. From Table 6-1 we obtain the estimate $\hat{\alpha} = 1.30$. The 95 percent confidence interval for a standardized stable distribution with $\alpha = 1.30$ is -6.25 to 6.25. Consequently, $C/\hat{s}(C)$ falls within the interval and is not starred.

Values of the χ^2 statistic above the .95 fractile (3.84) are also starred.

SUMMARY OF RESULTS

1. The means test rejects the pure expectations hypothesis. In most cases, the sample mean first difference is significantly different from zero. If this were the only test employed, the pure expectations hypothesis would certainly be rejected.

2. Most of the χ^2 values, which should be about unity if the sequence $(r_{j,t}, r_{j-1,t+1}, \ldots)$ is a random walk, are very significant. There are exceptions, of course. In particular, the forward rate sequences corresponding to maturities 1, 2, 3, 19, 21, 22, and 23 are well approximated by random walks (with drift) during this sample period.

3. In contrast to the χ^2 tests, only maturity 13 has a covariance significantly different from zero at the 95 percent level of significance. Most of these covariances are not significantly different from zero even at considerably lower levels of significance. At the 90 percent level, only maturity 8 and maturity 12 of part 2 and maturity 6 of part 1 are added to the list of covariances different from zero. On the basis of this test, the pure expectations hypothesis would not be rejected.

NONPARAMETRIC COVARIANCE TESTS

As a check on the parametric covariance tests, the data have been split into subperiods. Signs of the sample covariances in these subperiods are given in Table 6-11. In part 1 of the table, the period October 1949 through December 1964 was divided into 24 nonoverlapping subperiods of 31 observations each. For this period, only the maturities 1-11 were available. In part 2 of the table, the period March 1959 through December 1964 was divided into 16 nonoverlapping subperiods of 17 observations each. The criterion for division was simply to make the number of observations in each subperiod match the number of subperiods as closely as possible and still include most of the observations for the entire period. From October 1949 through December 1964, 796 observations are available. Hence, 796 $- (24)(31 + 2) = 4$ observations in December 1964 were not used.[26]

Each subperiod can be regarded as an independent observation. If the true covariance is zero and the sampling distribution of the covariance is symmetric, the number of subperiods with positive covariances, n^+, has a binomial

TABLE 6-11   Nonparametric Tests of the Pure Expectations Hypothesis. Signs of Sample Covariances in Subperiods. U.S. Treasury Bill Forward Rate Changes, Weekly Observations, October 1949-December 1964

Subperiod Starting Date	Subperiod Number	Maturity											Total +
		1	2	3	4	5	6	7	8	9	10	11	
10-18-49	1	−	+	−	−	+	−	−	−	+	−	−	3
6-6-50	2	−	−	−	−	−	−	−	−	−	−	−	0
1-23-51	3	+	+	−	+	−	−	+	−	−	−	−	4
9-11-51	4	−	−	−	−	−	−	−	−	+	−	−	1
2-29-52	5	−	−	−	−	−	−	−	−	−	−	−	0
12-16-52	6	−	−	−	−	+	−	−	−	−	−	−	1
8-4-53	7	+	+	−	−	−	−	−	−	−	−	−	2
3-23-54	8	+	−	+	−	−	−	−	−	−	−	−	2
11-1-54	9	+	−	−	+	−	−	−	−	−	−	−	2
6-21-55	10	−	−	−	−	−	−	+	−	−	−	−	1
2-7-56	11	−	−	+	+	−	−	−	−	−	−	−	2
9-25-56	12	+	+	+	−	−	−	+	−	−	−	−	4
5-14-57	13	−	+	−	−	−	−	−	−	+	−	−	2
12-30-57	14	−	+	+	+	−	−	−	−	−	−	−	3
9-19-58	15	+	+	+	−	−	+	−	−	−	+	−	5
4-7-59	16	+	+	+	−	−	+	−	−	−	−	−	4
11-24-59	17	−	+	+	−	+	−	−	−	−	−	−	3
7-12-60	18	+	+	+	−	−	−	+	−	+	−	−	5
2-28-61	19	+	−	−	−	−	−	−	−	−	−	+	2
10-17-61	20	+	+	−	−	−	−	−	−	−	−	−	2
6-5-62	21	−	+	+	−	−	−	−	−	−	−	−	2
1-22-63	22	+	−	−	−	−	−	−	−	−	−	−	1
9-10-63	23	−	+	−	−	+	−	−	−	−	+	−	3
4-28-64	24	+	−	+	−	−	−	−	−	+	−	−	3
Total +		12	13	10	4	4	2	4	0	5	3	1	57

Part 1. October 1949-December 1964   N = 31

Continued on following page

TABLE 6-11 (continued)

	Part 2.		March 1959-December 1964									$N = 17$				
Subperiod Starting Date	3-17-59	7-28-59	12-8-59	4-19-60	8-30-60	1-10-61	5-23-61	10-3-61	2-13-61	6-26-62	11-5-62	3-19-63	7-30-63	12-10-63	4-21-64	9-1-64	
Subperiod Number	1	2	3	4	5	6	7	8	9	10	11	12	13	14	15	16	
Maturity																	Total +
1	+	+	−	−	−	+	+	+	+	−	−	+	−	+	+	−	9
2	+	+	+	−	+	−	−	+	+	+	+	−	−	+	+	−	10
3	−	+	+	+	+	−	+	−	+	−	+	−	+	−	−	+	9
4	+	−	−	+	−	−	−	−	−	+	−	−	−	+	−	+	5
5	−	−	+	−	−	−	−	−	−	−	−	−	+	−	+	−	3
6	+	+	−	−	−	−	−	−	−	−	+	+	−	−	+	−	5
7	−	−	−	+	+	−	−	−	−	−	+	−	−	−	−	−	3
8	−	−	−	−	−	−	+	−	−	−	−	−	−	−	+	−	2
9	+	−	−	−	+	−	−	−	−	−	−	−	−	−	−	+	3
10	−	−	−	−	−	−	−	−	+	−	−	−	−	+	−	+	3
11	−	+	−	−	−	+	−	−	−	+	−	−	+	−	−	−	4
12	−	−	−	−	−	−	−	−	−	−	−	−	−	−	−	−	0
13	−	−	−	−	−	−	−	−	−	−	−	−	−	−	−	−	0
14	−	+	−	−	−	+	+	+	−	−	−	−	+	−	−	−	5
15	+	−	−	−	−	−	−	−	−	−	−	−	−	−	−	−	1
16	−	−	−	−	+	+	−	−	−	−	−	−	−	+	−	−	3
17	−	+	−	−	−	−	+	+	−	−	−	−	−	−	−	+	4
18	+	−	−	−	+	+	−	−	+	+	−	−	+	−	−	−	6
19	−	+	+	−	−	+	+	−	−	−	−	−	+	−	−	−	5
20	−	+	−	+	−	+	−	−	−	−	−	−	−	−	−	−	3
21	−	+	−	−	−	−	−	−	−	+	−	−	+	−	−	−	3
22	−	−	+	−	−	+	−	−	−	−	+	−	−	−	+	−	4
23	−	+	+	+	+	+	−	+	−	−	−	−	−	−	−	+	7
24	−	−	−	−	−	+	−	−	−	−	−	−	−	+	−	−	2
Total +	7	11	6	5	7	10	5	6	5	6	5	1	8	6	5	6	99

distribution with probability of success, $p = \dfrac{1}{2}$. For each maturity, j, the 95 percent acceptance interval on n_j^+ is given by

$$18 > n_j^+ > 7$$

for part 1 of the table (where the number of independent subperiods is 24) and by

$$13 > n_j^+ > 4$$

for part 2 of the table (where the number of subperiods is 16).

Part 1 of Table 6-11 disagrees with the corresponding parametric covariance tests in part 1 of Table 6-10. Counts for maturities 4-11 in Table 6-11 all lie outside the 95 percent acceptance interval for the binomial distribution with $p = \frac{1}{2}$. In part 2, counts for maturities 5, 7-13, 15-17, 20-22, and 24 also lie outside the acceptance interval.

In contrast, the inferences about covariance drawn from the nonparametric tests of Table 6-11 agree almost perfectly with the inferences about serial *dependence* measured by the χ^2 values of Table 6-10, parts 1 and 2. In only four cases, maturities 14, 18, 21, and 22, are the conclusions different.

This suggests that the parametric tests based on stable distribution theory are deficient. Perhaps the estimates of α and s are poorer than we had believed. On the other hand, it could suggest that the nonparametric covariance test is faulty, perhaps because the distribution of the sample covariance is asymmetric.

CONCLUSIONS ABOUT THE HYPOTHESIS

The means tests and the nonparametric covariance tests reject the pure expectations hypothesis. The parametric covariance tests do not reject it. However, even if the parametric covariance tests were correct, the absence of serial correlation would not necessarily save the pure expectations hypothesis because the other term structure hypotheses are consistent under certain conditions with *both* zero serial correlation in forward rate changes *and* with nonzero mean forward rate changes. For example, if the stationary market segmentation hypothesis were correct and if $L_{j+1,t-1} > L_{j,t-1}$, an examination of the equation in the first row of Table 6-9 shows that the mean forward rate change would be negative, as most of the sample values are; and, if $L_{j+1,t-1} - L_{j,t-1}$ were a constant over all t, the mean forward rate change would be serially uncorrelated.

A Digression on Liquidity Premiums[27]

Since the average forward rate changes are nonzero, sample estimates of liquidity premiums are necessarily nonzero. It would be worthwhile knowing their magnitudes. Although individual liquidity premiums cannot be observed directly, averages can be calculated from the average forward rate changes.

Table 6-9 gives the equation $E_{t-1}(r_{j,t} - r_{j+1,t-1}) = L_{j,t-1} - L_{j+1,t-1}$ for the liquidity preference or the stationary market segmentation hypothesis. Since $L_{1,t} = 0$ for all t, an estimate of $L_{n,t}$ is given by

$$\hat{L}_{n,t} = \sum_{j=2}^{n} \overline{(r_{j,t} - r_{j-1,t+1})}$$

where $\overline{r_{j,t} - r_{j-1,t+1}}$ refers to the .5 truncated sample mean of the forward rate first difference. Values of $\hat{L}_{n,t}$ are given in Table 6-12.

TABLE 6-12   Average Liquidity Premiums, U.S. Treasury Bills, 1949-1964

October 1949-December 1964		March 1959-December 1964			
Maturity, n (weeks)	L_n (%/annum)	Maturity, n (weeks)	L_n (%/annum)	Maturity, n (weeks)	L_n (%/annum)
1	0	1	0	13	.562
2	.0159	2	.00704	14	.0403
3	.0565	3	.0555	15	.0696
4	.129	4	.168	16	.142
5	.208	5	.291	17	.175
6	.240	6	.323	18	.189
7	.253	7	.347	19	.256
8	.274	8	.383	20	.262
9	.303	9	.445	21	.296
10	.257	10	.427	22	.305
11	.231	11	.396	23	.310
12	.258	12	.414	24	.328
				25	.365

These values are in agreement with one contention of the liquidity preference hypothesis since they are uniformly positive. They disagree, however, with a second contention that liquidity premiums increase monotonically with maturity. The average liquidity premiums for maturities 14-21 are much lower than those for maturities 6-13.

The Time-Dependent Market Segmentation Hypothesis

This section examines the behavior of the yield change, $R_{j,t} - R_{j+1,t-1}$. Its sample mean and serial covariance will be calculated and tested for deviations from zero. Its serial dependence will be tested.[28] These tests are identical to those conducted for the forward rate change, $r_{j,t} - r_{j+1,t-1}$ (see Table 6-10 and its description) so the description of the tests will not be repeated here. Table 6-13 provides the

TABLE 6-13   Tests of the Time-Dependent Market Segmentation Hypothesis with Sample Means and Serial Covariances of $R_{n,t} - R_{n+1,t-1}$, U.S. Treasury Bill Yield Changes, Weekly Observations, October 1949-December 1964

Maturity (weeks)	Mean (%/annum) 10^2	$\dfrac{\mid \text{Mean} \mid}{\text{Standard Error}}$	C (%/annum)^2 $\times 10^3$	$\dfrac{\mid C \mid}{\hat{s}(C)}$	χ^2	N
		Part 1.	October 1949-December 1964			
1	−.911	1.68	−.962	.720	.428	794
2	−1.69*	3.66	1.24	.943	.464	794
3	−2.73*	6.42	2.20	2.00	1.32	794
4	−3.22*	7.85	2.89	3.03	4.00*	794
5	−2.56*	7.14	3.13	3.32	8.92*	794
6	−2.60*	7.63	3.11	3.28	8.99*	794
7	−1.74*	5.38	2.80	3.79	4.59*	794
8	−1.58*	5.74	2.33	2.85	7.63*	794
9	−1.04*	3.55	1.95	2.99	3.54	794
10	−.378	1.47	1.46	1.85	1.99	794
11	−.414	1.71	1.00	1.14	.930	768
		Part 2.	March 1959-December 1964			
1	−.930	1.28	−.519	.202	.00599	303
2	−1.93*	2.71	2.62	1.33	4.47*	303
3	−3.82*	5.80	3.59	2.41	1.06	303
4	−4.56*	7.91	4.44	2.41	8.44*	303
5	−3.28*	6.00	4.72	3.51	7.72*	303
6	−2.53*	5.05	4.56	3.42	11.2*	303
7	−2.36*	5.27	3.81	2.86	8.45*	303
8	−2.31*	5.89	3.16	2.55	4.89*	303
9	−1.58*	4.44	2.80	2.37	4.75*	303
10	−.963*	2.84	1.88	1.52	3.24	303
11	−.805	2.40	1.42	.921	1.28	303
12	−1.67*	4.57	−1.17	.601	.536	303
13	2.07*	4.89	.658	.423	.165	303
14	−.513	1.31	.461	.361	.450	303
15	−1.11*	3.27	1.41	1.51	1.08	303
16	−1.11*	3.32	1.28	1.44	.484	303
17	−1.13*	3.44	1.18	1.36	1.40	303
18	−1.55*	5.49	1.66	1.68	3.23	303
19	−1.44*	5.10	1.52	1.68	.111	303
20	−1.39*	4.67	1.15	1.21	.460	303
21	−1.25*	4.43	1.58	1.59	1.27	303
22	−.964*	3.09	1.77	1.60	5.26*	303
23	−.798*	2.38	1.82	1.85	3.53	303
24	−.860*	2.44	1.78	1.52	1.60	290

results. The table is separated into two parts in the same manner as Table 6-10 and the labels are self-explanatory.

The results are very similar to those for the pure expectations hypothesis. There is no evidence of serial correlation and except for maturities 4-8 there is not even any evidence of serial dependence. On the other hand, the .5 truncated sample mean yield change is significantly different from zero (at the 95 percent confidence level) in almost every. case.[29]

Again, as a cross-check on the covariances, the data were split into subperiods. Signs of the covariances in these subperiods are reported in Table 6-14. The 95 percent acceptance intervals on the number of positive covariances, counting across subperiods for each maturity, are

$$18 > n^+ > 7$$

for part 1 of the table ($N = 24$) and

$$13 > n^+ > 4$$

for part 2 of the table ($N = 16$) under the null hypothesis that a positive covariance has a probability of occurrence $p = \frac{1}{2}$. Maturities 5-9 of part 1 of Table 6-14 are outside this interval. Again, as in the case for forward rate changes, this conflicts with the parametric tests of covariance given in part 1 of Table 6-13. Again, it agrees more with the χ^2 tests of dependence (in four of the five cases). However, part 2 of Table 6-14 is in perfect agreement with its parametric counterpart in part 2 of Table 6-13. None of the covariances in either case are significantly different from zero at the 95 percent level of significance.

TABLE 6-14   Nonparametric Tests of the Time-Dependent Market
Segmentation Hypothesis, Signs of Sample Covariances
in Subperiods, U.S. Treasury Bill Yield Changes,
Weekly Observations, October 1949-December 1964

Part 1.		October 1949-December 1964								N = 31			
Subperiod Starting Date	Subperiod Number	Maturity											
		1	2	3	4	5	6	7	8	9	10	11	Total +
10-18-49	1	−	+	−	−	+	−	−	−	+	−	−	3
6-6-50	2	−	−	−	−	−	−	−	−	−	−	−	0
1-23-51	3	+	+	+	+	+	+	+	−	+	+	−	9
9-11-51	4	+	+	+	+	+	+	+	+	+	+	+	11
2-29-52	5	−	−	−	−	−	−	−	−	−	−	−	0
12-16-52	6	−	−	−	−	+	−	−	+	−	+	+	4
8-4-53	7	+	−	−	−	+	+	+	+	+	+	+	8
3-23-54	8	+	−	+	−	+	+	+	+	+	+	+	9
11-1-54	9	+	+	+	+	+	+	+	+	+	+	+	11
6-21-55	10	+	+	+	+	+	+	+	+	+	+	+	11
2-7-56	11	−	−	+	+	+	−	+	+	−	−	−	5
9-25-56	12	+	+	+	+	+	+	+	+	+	+	−	10
5-14-57	13	−	−	−	−	+	+	+	+	+	−	−	5
12-30-57	14	+	+	+	+	+	+	+	+	+	+	+	11
8-19-58	15	−	−	−	−	−	+	+	+	+	+	−	5
4-7-59	16	−	+	+	+	+	+	+	+	+	+	+	10
11-24-59	17	−	+	+	+	+	+	+	+	+	+	+	10
7-12-60	18	+	+	+	+	+	+	+	+	+	+	−	10
2-28-61	19	+	+	+	+	+	+	+	+	+	+	+	11
10-17-61	20	−	+	+	+	+	+	+	+	+	+	+	10
6-5-62	21	−	+	+	+	+	+	+	+	+	+	+	10
1-22-63	22	−	−	−	−	+	−	+	+	−	−	−	3
9-10-63	23	+	+	+	−	+	+	−	+	−	−	−	6
4-28-64	24	−	+	+	+	−	+	+	+	+	+	+	9
Total +		11	15	16	14	20	18	19	20	18	17	13	181

Continued on following page

CONCLUSIONS ABOUT THE TIME-DEPENDENT MARKET
SEGMENTATION HYPOTHESIS

This hypothesis implies

$$E_{t-1}(\widetilde{R}_{j,t} - R_{j+1,t-1}) = A_j$$

TABLE 6-14 (continued)

	Part 2.				March 1959-December 1964								N = 17				
Subperiod Starting Date	3-17-59	7-28-59	12-8-59	4-19-60	8-30-60	1-10-61	5-23-61	10-3-61	2-13-62	6-26-62	11-5-62	3-19-63	7-30-63	12-10-63	4-21-64	9-1-64	
Subperiod Number	1	2	3	4	5	6	7	8	9	10	11	12	13	14	15	16	
Maturity																	Total +
1	−	−	−	−	+	+	+	−	+	+	−	−	−	−	−	−	5
2	−	+	+	−	+	−	+	+	+	+	−	−	−	+	+	−	9
3	−	+	+	−	+	+	+	+	+	+	−	−	−	−	−	−	8
4	−	+	+	+	+	+	+	+	+	+	−	+	−	−	+	+	12
5	−	+	+	+	+	+	+	+	+	+	−	+	−	−	−	−	10
6	−	+	+	+	+	+	+	+	−	+	−	+	+	−	+	−	11
7	−	+	+	+	+	+	+	+	−	+	−	+	+	−	−	−	10
8	−	+	−	+	+	+	+	+	−	+	−	+	+	−	−	−	9
9	+	+	+	+	+	+	+	+	−	+	−	+	−	−	+	−	11
10	+	+	+	+	+	+	+	+	−	+	−	+	−	−	−	−	10
11	+	+	−	+	−	+	+	+	−	+	−	+	−	−	−	+	9
12	−	−	−	−	+	+	+	+	−	+	−	+	−	−	−	−	6
13	+	−	+	−	+	+	+	+	−	+	−	+	−	−	−	+	9
14	−	+	+	−	+	+	+	+	−	+	−	−	−	−	−	+	8
15	−	+	+	−	+	+	+	+	−	+	−	+	−	−	−	+	9
16	−	+	+	−	+	+	+	+	−	+	−	+	−	−	−	−	8
17	−	+	+	−	+	+	+	+	−	+	−	+	−	−	+	−	9
18	−	+	+	−	+	+	+	+	−	+	−	+	−	−	+	+	10
19	−	+	+	−	+	+	+	−	−	+	−	+	−	−	+	−	8
20	−	+	+	−	+	+	+	+	−	+	−	+	−	−	−	+	9
21	−	+	+	+	+	+	+	+	−	+	−	+	−	+	−	+	11
22	−	+	+	+	+	+	+	+	−	+	−	+	−	−	−	+	10
23	−	+	+	+	+	+	+	+	−	+	−	+	−	−	−	+	10
24	−	+	+	+	+	+	+	+	−	+	−	+	−	−	−	+	10
Total +	4	21	20	12	23	23	24	22	5	24	0	20	3	2	7	11	221

(cf. Table 6-9). The empirical evidence suggests that (1) A_j is negative on average, (2) A_j does not increase as fast as j (this is evidenced by the sample mean of $R_{j,t} - R_{j+1,t-1}$ being highest for maturities 3-5), and (3) A_j is roughly constant over time except, perhaps, for maturities 3-9. This conclusion follows from the serial dependence and correlation statistics being close to zero for maturities other than 3-9.

In summary, the time-dependent market segmentation hypothesis fits the data quite well except for maturities in the 3-9-week range. In the 3-9-week range, the hypothesis does not fit the data. The nonparametric covariance tests reject the hypothesis for the period October 1949-December 1964 and the χ^2 tests show that yield changes corresponding to these maturities are serially dependent. The sample covariances are also much larger for these maturities than for other maturities. It is no coincidence that the average values of A_j are larger for these maturities than for any others. A_j appears to play a more important role in this maturity range and its size probably fluctuates more widely over time, thus introducing more serial dependence into the yield changes.

The Stationary Market Segmentation Hypothesis and the Liquidity Preference Hypothesis

The change in one-period yields, $R_{1,t} - R_{1,t-1}$, plays a crucial role in the dynamic equations of these hypotheses. Table 6-9 (column 3, row 3) gives the equation

$$E_{t-1}(\widetilde{R}_{j,t} - R_{j,t-1}) = \frac{1}{j}(r_{j+1,t-1} - L_{j+1,t-1} - R_{1,t-1})$$

for the expected change in the j-period yield. By definition, $r_{j+1,t-1} - L_{j+1,t-1} = E_{t-1}(\widetilde{R}_{1,t+j-1})$. See equation (3-10). Consequently, the yield change equation can be rewritten

$$E_{t-1}(\widetilde{R}_{j,t} - R_{j,t-1}) = \frac{1}{j}[E_{t-1}(\widetilde{R}_{1,t+j-1}) - R_{1,t-1}]$$

which shows that the expected j-period yield change and the serial correlation in the j-period yield change is proportional to the expected one-period yield change over j periods and the serial correlation in the one-period changes (provided, of course, that the stationary market segmentation hypothesis is valid).

[Note that if the sequence $(R_{1,t}, R_{1,t+1}, \ldots)$ should happen to be a martingale, all sequences such as $(R_{j,t}, R_{j,t+1}, \ldots)$ will also be submartingales.]

EMPIRICAL EVIDENCE OF SERIAL CORRELATION IN $R_{1,t-1}$

Table 6-15 presents serial correlation coefficients for the variable $R_{1,t} - R_{1,t-1}$ and for several lags. The sampling distribution of the correlation coefficient is unknown when the variates being correlated are nonnormal stable, and so

TABLE 6-15 Serial Correlation Coefficients Between One-Period Yield Changes, U.S. Treasury Bills, 1949-1964

Lag (weeks)	Correlation Coefficient[a]
1	−.0902
2	−.0889
3	−.0894
4	.0120
5	−.0150
6	−.0529
7	.0171
8	−.0426
9	.0609
10	−.0953

[a]The sample sizes for the coefficients range from 794 for a lag of 1 to 785 for a lag of 10.

definite inferences cannot be drawn from these results. However, the small size of the coefficients indicates that $(R_{1,t},\ R_{1,t+1},\ \ldots)$ fairly approximates a submartingale sequence. Also, examination of Table 6-16 shows that $R_{1,t} - R_{1,t-1}$ has an expected value insignificantly different from zero. Thus, the sequence of one-period spot yields is close to a *pure* martingale.

EMPIRICAL EVIDENCE ABOUT $R_{j,t} - R_{j,t-1}$

Since the one-period yield sequence seems to approximate a pure martingale, the stationary market segmentation hypothesis and the liquidity preference hypothesis imply that $R_{j,t} - R_{j,t-1}$ has an expected value of zero and is serially uncorrelated. Hence we now report this variable's sample means, sample covariances, and χ^2 statistics from two-way contingency tables. Unfortunately, the parametric scale measure of the sample covariance no longer applies. In the previous tests, the sample covariance was of the form

$$C_{U_t V_t} = \frac{1}{N} \sum_{t=1}^{N} u_t v_t$$

(where u_t and v_t are deviations about sample means), so that the u's could be assumed nonstochastic and a conditional (on the u's) measure of the scale of $C_{U_t V_t}$ was possible, namely,

$$\hat{s}(C_{U_t V_t} \mid \mathbf{U}) = \hat{s}(\widetilde{V}) \left(\sum_{t=1}^{N} \left| \frac{u_t}{N} \right|^{\hat{\alpha}} \right)^{1/\hat{\alpha}}$$

Now, however, the process involves a lagged variable since $U_t = V_{t-1}$, and we would have

$$\hat{s}(C_{U_t V_t} \mid \mathbf{U}) = \hat{s}(C_{V_{t-1} V_t} \mid V_1, V_2, \ldots, V_{N-1})$$

so that V_N would be the only "nonstochastic" observation. The tables continue to report $|C|/\hat{s}(C)$ where

$$\hat{s}(C) = \hat{s}(\widetilde{V}) \left(\sum_{t=2}^{N} \left| \frac{v_{t-1}}{(N-1)} \right|^{\hat{\alpha}} \right)^{1/\hat{\alpha}}$$

but no inferences will be drawn using this statistic. Instead, we shall rely on the nonparametric covariance tests.

Table 6-16 reports the results. The sample mean[30] is supposed to be zero if the hypotheses are valid, and it is not significantly different from zero for 33 maturities.[31]

The serial covariance and dependence tests also support the hypotheses very well. The sample covariances are very close to zero, and only 6 of the 39 χ^2 values are above the .95 fractile. This supports the conclusion that the yield changes are serially independent (and, of course, uncorrelated).

The nonparametric tests of serial covariance derived from splitting the data into subsamples are reported in Table 6-17. These results suggest that:

1. The serial covariance in one-period yield changes is significantly negative for the period October 1949-December 1964 (part 1 of Table 6-17) but not significantly different from zero in part 2 of the table (March 1959-December 1964).

2. The serial covariances for maturities 4 and 6 are significantly positive for part 1 but not for part 2.

(The significance level was 95 percent in these tests. See p. 93).

In summary, these hypotheses generally seem to fit the data very well.

TABLE 6-16 Tests of the Stationary Market Segmentation Hypothesis and the Liquidity Preference Hypothesis with Sample Means and Serial Covariances of $R_{n,t} - R_{n,t-1}$, U.S. Treasury Bill Yield Changes, Weekly Observations, October 1949-December 1964

Maturity, n (weeks)	Mean (%/annum) $\times 10^2$	$\dfrac{|\text{Mean}|}{\text{Standard Error}}$	C (%/annum)^2 $\times 10^3$	$\dfrac{|C|}{\hat{s}(C)}$	χ^2	N
	Part 1.	*October 1949-December 1964*				
1	−.219	.414	−3.24	1.43	3.27	794
2	−.245	.477	−.929	.470	.137	794
3	.199	.379	1.85	1.63	.559	794
4	.136	.284	2.98	2.33	.0498	794
5	.0572	.140	1.84	1.39	.00267	794
6	.0332	.0924	3.09	2.44	4.52*	794
7	.386	1.18	2.12	1.99	1.58	794
8	.507	1.72	2.09	1.86	3.93*	794
9	.569	1.85	.794	.820	.202	794
10	.850*	3.10	1.09	1.22	.0527	794
11	.646*	2.67	1.01	1.12	.886	794
12	.768*	2.95	.342	.389	.0466	794
13	.648*	2.25	.452	.517	.248	723
	Part 2.	*March 1959-December 1964*				
1	−1.15	1.37	−5.19	1.21	3.33	303
2	−.784	1.01	−.513	.148	.713	303
3	−.243	.302	4.77	2.52	7.13*	303
4	−.487	.625	4.71	2.25	.667	303
5	−.0739	.131	3.69	1.66	1.58	303
6	.247	.441	4.97	2.82	6.01*	303
7	.401	.801	3.84	2.72	5.97*	303
8	.609	1.55	2.24	1.09	3.89*	303
9	.357	.876	.753	.564	.0296	303
10	.581	1.48	.994	.727	.372	303
11	.399	1.10	1.25	1.04	1.21	303
12	.363	.994	−.328	.191	.400	303
13	.426	1.09	.355	.366	.00446	303
14	.378	.957	−.989	.639	.0917	303
15	.114	.271	.284	.314	.532	303
16	.398	1.02	.294	.380	.718	303
17	.156	.402	.989	1.33	.0816	303
18	.325	.894	.754	.803	.162	303
19	.316	.809	1.78	2.33	.204	303
20	.314	.967	1.29	1.33	.00258	303
21	.265	.788	1.52	1.73	.454	303
22	.502	1.76	.613	.536	.554	303
23	.671*	2.17	.789	.607	1.17	303
24	.648*	1.97	2.45	2.32	.844	303
25	.563	1.44	.866	.631	.904	303
26	.268	.683	.890	.503	.420	266

Conclusions About the "Best" Term Structure Hypothesis

We have examined the behavior of three interest rate changes, $r_{j,t} - r_{j+1,t-1}$, $R_{j,t} - R_{j+1,t-1}$, and $R_{j,t} - R_{j,t-1}$, which provide evidence about the reality of hypotheses of the term structure. The conclusions are:

1. The pure expectations hypothesis can be firmly rejected. The forward rate changes, $r_{j,t} - r_{j+1,t-1}$, do not have expected values of zero and *are* serially correlated.

2. The other two hypotheses fit the data fairly well, although the test results are ambiguous in some cases.

3. The time-dependent market segmentation hypothesis does not seem to be valid for maturities of from 3 to 9 weeks since there is serial correlation in $R_{j,t} - R_{j+1,t-1}$ at these maturities.

4. The stationary market segmentation hypothesis and the liquidity preference hypothesis are well supported by the absence of serial correlation in $R_{j,t} - R_{j,t-1}$ for all j. Indeed, the χ^2 tests show that R_j closely approximates a random walk over time. In addition, the means test strongly supports the contention of the hypothesis that $E_{t-1}(\widetilde{R}_{j,t} - R_{j,t-1}) = 0$.

EFFICIENCY OF THE U.S. TREASURY BILL MARKET

Chapter 2 of this investigation suggested that price changes in an efficient market are serially uncorrelated. Before testing this proposition with actual price changes, however, some consideration must be given to the possibility that the *expected* price change is not a constant over time. Spurious positive serial dependence can be introduced

TABLE 6-17 Nonparametric Tests of the Stationary Market Segmentation Hypothesis or the Liquidity Preference Hypothesis, Signs of Sample Covariances in Subperiods, U.S. Treasury Bill Yield Changes, Weekly Observations, October 1949-December 1964

Part 1.		*October 1949-December 1964*								*N* = 31					

Subperiod Starting Date	Subperiod Number	Maturity													Total +
		1	2	3	4	5	6	7	8	9	10	11	12	13	
10-18-49	1	−	−	−	+	−	+	−	−	−	−	−	−	+	3
6-6-50	2	−	−	−	−	−	−	−	−	−	−	−	−	−	0
1-23-51	3	+	+	+	+	−	+	+	−	−	−	+	+	−	8
9-11-51	4	−	−	+	+	−	+	+	+	+	+	+	−	+	9
2-29-52	5	−	−	−	−	−	−	−	−	−	−	−	−	−	0
12-16-52	6	−	−	−	−	−	−	−	−	−	+	−	+	−	2
8-4-53	7	−	−	−	+	−	+	+	+	+	+	+	+	+	9
3-23-54	8	−	−	−	+	+	+	+	+	+	+	+	+	+	10
11-1-54	9	+	+	+	+	+	+	+	+	+	+	+	+	+	13
6-21-55	10	−	+	+	+	+	+	+	+	+	+	+	+	+	12
2-7-56	11	−	−	−	−	−	+	−	+	−	−	−	+	−	3
9-25-56	12	+	+	+	+	−	+	+	+	−	+	−	−	−	8
5-14-57	13	−	−	−	+	−	+	−	−	−	−	−	−	−	2
12-30-57	14	+	+	+	+	+	+	+	+	+	+	+	+	+	13
8-19-58	15	−	−	−	+	+	−	−	+	−	−	−	−	−	3
4-7-59	16	−	+	+	+	+	+	+	+	+	−	+	−	−	9
11-24-59	17	−	−	+	+	+	+	+	+	−	+	+	+	−	9
7-12-60	18	−	+	+	+	+	+	+	+	+	−	+	−	+	10
2-28-61	19	−	−	+	+	+	+	+	+	−	+	−	+	−	8
10-17-61	20	−	−	+	−	+	+	+	+	+	+	+	+	+	10
6-5-62	21	−	+	+	+	+	+	+	−	+	−	−	+	−	8
1-22-63	22	−	−	−	−	+	+	+	+	−	−	+	−	−	5
9-10-63	23	−	−	+	+	+	−	−	+	−	−	−	−	−	4
4-28-64	24	−	−	−	+	+	−	+	−	+	+	+	+	+	8
Total +		4	8	13	18	14	18	16	16	11	12	13	13	10	166

Continued on following page

into the data by a shifting mean without implying the existence of abnormally profitable returns to mechanistic trading rules. Now, we have tested three term structure theories and are ready to exploit their implications for

TABLE 6-17 (continued)

	Part 2. March 1959-December 1964 N = 17																
Subperiod Starting Date	3-17-59	7-28-59	12-8-59	4-19-60	8-30-60	1-10-61	5-23-61	10-3-61	2-13-62	6-26-62	11-5-62	3-19-63	7-30-63	12-10-63	4-21-64	9-1-64	
Subperiod Number	1	2	3	4	5	6	7	8	9	10	11	12	13	14	15	16	
Maturity																	Total +
1	−	−	−	−	+	−	−	−	+	+	−	−	−	−	+	−	4
2	−	+	+	−	+	−	−	−	+	+	+	−	+	−	−	+	8
3	+	+	+	−	+	+	+	−	+	+	+	−	+	+	+	−	12
4	−	+	+	−	+	+	+	+	−	+	+	−	+	−	+	−	10
5	+	+	+	−	+	+	+	+	−	+	−	−	+	−	+	−	10
6	−	+	+	−	+	+	+	+	+	+	−	+	−	+	−	+	11
7	−	+	+	+	+	+	+	+	+	+	+	+	−	−	−	+	12
8	−	+	+	−	+	+	+	+	−	+	−	+	+	+	−	−	10
9	−	+	−	+	+	−	+	+	−	+	+	+	−	−	−	−	8
10	−	+	+	−	+	+	+	+	−	+	−	+	−	−	−	−	8
11	−	+	+	+	+	−	+	−	−	+	−	+	−	−	−	−	7
12	−	−	−	−	−	+	+	+	−	+	−	+	−	−	−	+	6
13	−	−	−	−	+	+	−	+	−	+	−	+	−	−	−	+	6
14	+	−	+	−	−	+	−	+	−	+	−	+	−	−	−	+	7
15	+	+	+	−	−	+	+	+	−	+	−	−	−	−	−	+	8
16	−	+	+	−	−	−	+	+	−	+	−	+	−	+	−	+	8
17	−	+	+	−	+	+	−	+	−	+	−	+	−	−	−	−	7
18	+	−	+	−	+	−	+	−	−	+	−	+	−	−	+	−	7
19	−	+	+	−	+	+	+	+	−	+	−	+	−	−	+	−	9
20	−	+	+	−	+	+	+	+	−	+	−	+	−	−	−	−	8
21	−	+	+	−	+	+	+	−	−	+	−	+	−	+	−	+	9
22	−	−	+	+	+	−	+	−	−	+	−	+	−	−	−	−	6
23	−	−	+	+	+	+	+	−	−	+	−	+	−	−	−	+	8
24	−	+	+	+	+	+	+	−	−	+	−	+	−	−	−	+	9
25	−	+	+	+	+	+	+	−	−	+	−	+	−	−	−	+	9
26	−	+	+	−	+	+	−	+	−	−	−	+	−	−	−	+	7
Total +	5	19	22	7	22	19	20	16	5	25	5	20	5	5	6	13	214

adjusting and testing the serial behavior of U.S. Treasury bill price changes.

The last row of Table 6-9 provides equations for the behavior of market price changes under each of the term structure hypotheses. These equations are:

1. The pure expectations hypothesis:

$$E_{t-1}[\log(\widetilde{p}_{j,t}/p_{j+1,t-1})] = R_{1,t-1} \qquad (6\text{-}11)$$

2. The time-dependent market segmentation hypothesis:

$$E_{t-1}[\log(\widetilde{p}_{j,t}/p_{j+1,t-1})] = R_{j+1,t-1} - jA_j \qquad (6\text{-}12)$$

3. The stationary market segmentation hypothesis or the liquidity preference hypothesis:

$$E_{t-1}[\log(\widetilde{p}_{j,t}/p_{j+1,t-1})] = R_{1,t-1} + L_{j+1,t-1} \qquad (6\text{-}13)$$

The *expected* log price relative in each case depends on the *current* one-period yield, and for the second and third hypotheses it also includes liquidity premiums.[32] We must expect this nonstationarity in the expected price change to induce some positive serial dependence in observed price changes.

Empirical Results

This section presents empirical measures of the serial *dependence* in three different price relatives:

1. The unadjusted price relative
2. The price relative adjusted for the one-period yield
3. The price relative adjusted for the one-period yield and the liquidity premium

The first-order serial covariance and the two-way contingency table χ^2 test of serial dependence will be given in each case. (The only difference in the χ^2 test from similar tests for dependence in yield changes is that the contingency table here is divided by the .5 truncated sample mean rather than by zero.)

UNADJUSTED PRICE RELATIVES

First, for comparison with other studies, the serial dependence in the unadjusted log price relative, $\log_e(p_{j,t}/p_{j+1,t-1})$, is given. This sample covariance is

$$\frac{1}{N-2} \sum_{t=1}^{N-2} \left[\log\left(\frac{p_{j,t}}{p_{j+1,t-1}}\right) - \overline{\log\left(\frac{p_{j,t}}{p_{j+1,t-1}}\right)} \right] \left[\log\left(\frac{p_{j+1,t-1}}{p_{j+2,t-2}}\right) - \overline{\log\left(\frac{p_{j+1,t-1}}{p_{j+2,t-2}}\right)} \right]$$

where the bars refer to the .5 truncated sample means.

The results are tabulated under "unadjusted" in Table 6-18. (This table is broken into parts in the same manner as the tables in preceding sections; viz., part 1 reports maturities of 1-11 weeks from October 1949 through December 1964, and part 2 gives maturities 1-24 from March 1959 through December 1964.)

The χ^2 values of unadjusted log price relatives are almost large enough to be measured in milliards. (Recall that the two-way contingency table produces a χ^2 distribution with one degree of freedom under the null hypothesis.)

ADJUSTMENT FOR R_1

All three term structure theories suggest that the log price relative should be adjusted by at least the one-period yield before testing for serial dependence. (See the equations on p. 112.) Consequently, we now present the sample covariance

HUNT LIBRARY
CARNEGIE-MELLON UNIVERSITY

TABLE 6-18   Sample Serial Covariances of Log Price Relatives and Tests of Serial Dependence by Contingency Tables, U.S. Treasury Bills, Weekly Observations, 1949-1964[a]

Maturity, n (weeks)	Unadjusted Sample Covariance (%/annum)^2	χ^2	Adjusted for R_1 Sample Covariance (%/annum)^2	χ^2	Adjusted for R_{j+1} Sample Covariance (%/annum)^2	χ^2
\multicolumn{7}{c}{Part 1.   October 1949-December 1964}
1	.655	395	.00279	3.55	−.00192	.194
2	.698	359	.0157	2.96	.00746	.682
3	.773	298	.0459	18.4	.0265	2.74
4	.842	285	.0850	34.8	.0577	11.9
5	.890	242	.125	31.1	.0938	16.5
6	.959	237	.176	39.5	.131	22.0
7	1.04	241	.217	45.0	.157	18.1
8	1.09	228	.238	28.9	.167	7.08
9	1.10	214	.255	26.8	.175	2.52
10	1.07	180	.241	12.2	.161	.00479
11	1.06	158	.250	19.5	.132	.434
\multicolumn{7}{c}{Part 2.   March 1959-December 1964}
1	.354	136	.00585	2.34	−.00104	.00307
2	.364	98.9	.0294	3.13	.0157	1.73
3	.372	58.4	.0672	9.90	.0431	5.03
4	.390	53.3	.115	13.8	.0887	8.60
5	.426	49.7	.173	14.5	.142	12.8
6	.473	51.3	.234	22.2	.192	9.09
7	.501	62.3	.263	24.6	.213	16.3
8	.543	51.7	.290	16.5	.227	6.98
9	.587	35.0	.331	11.3	.252	.397
10	.534	35.0	.295	8.81	.207	.266
11	.549	33.6	.332	10.5	.187	.735
12	.119	3.63	−.213	.568	−.182	8.51
13	.442	7.29	.0649	.161	.120	.166
14	.381	6.68	.137	3.15	.0967	.389
15	.646	13.1	.444	8.38	.339	3.06
16	.687	9.28	.473	12.1	.347	4.76
17	.737	13.1	.542	16.6	.361	2.79
18	.978	16.6	.811	20.6	.568	6.11
19	.957	6.68	.797	16.4	.578	2.42
20	.867	8.58	.697	28.1	.482	5.85
21	1.18	9.27	1.00	19.3	.731	1.29
22	1.37	4.51	1.19	13.1	.896	3.17
23	1.48	3.60	1.33	7.29	1.00	3.17
24	1.63	3.13	1.44	4.51	1.07	.672

[a]Sample sizes are the same as in Table 6-13.

$$\text{cov}\left[\log\left(\frac{p_{j,t}}{p_{j+1,t-1}}\,e^{-R_{1,t-1}}\right),\,\log\left(\frac{p_{j+1,t-1}}{p_{j+2,t-2}}\,e^{-R_{1,t-2}}\right)\right]$$

and the corresponding χ^2 statistics from a two-way contingency table. These results are given under the heading "adjusted for R_1" in Table 6-18. The adjustment reduces χ^2 in all cases in part 1 and for maturities 1-15 of part 2. For these maturities, one can conclude that much of the serial dependence in adjusted log price relatives is accounted for by changes in the level of the one-period yield.

However, for maturities 16-24, adjusting the price relative by the one-period yield not only fails to lower χ^2 but it raises it, in many cases from an insignificant to a significant level.

ADJUSTMENT FOR LIQUIDITY PREMIUMS AND R_1

Although adjusting the log price relative by R_1 lowers the χ^2 values in many cases from its unadjusted level, nearly all the χ^2 values are still far out in the tail of the distribution under the null hypothesis. This is really not too surprising since we have already seen that the pure expectations hypothesis, which implies that the price relative should be adjusted by the one-period yield and *only* by the one-period yield [cf. equation (6-11)], fails to fit the data.

Since the other hypotheses fit the data better, their implications should be satisfied. The price relative should also be adjusted for a liquidity premium, per equation (6-12) or (6-13). Unfortunately, liquidity premiums are not directly measurable and it is necessary to substitute a proxy.

The easiest proxy to use is $R_{j+1,t-1}$. This comes from equation (6-12) for the time-dependent market segmentation hypothesis. Equation (6-12) indicates that the variable

$$\log_e[(p_{j,t}/p_{j+1,t-1})\exp(-R_{j+1,t-1})] \qquad (6\text{-}14)$$

is serially uncorrelated because $-jA_j$, the conditional expected value of (6-14), is a constant.

The column headed by "adjusted for R_{j+1}" in Table 6-18 gives the serial covariance and χ^2 values for the log price relative adjusted according to (6-14). In every case except maturities 12 and 13 of part 2, the χ^2 values are lower than the corresponding χ^2 values when the price relative is adjusted only by R_1. The χ^2 values are also lower than those for the unadjusted price relative except for maturity 12 of part 2. But most importantly, the χ^2 values are generally well within the range expected under the null hypothesis that the log price relative is serially independent. The exceptions are maturities 4-8. For these maturities, the adjusted price relative is serially dependent because the time-dependent market segmentation hypothesis of the term structure, whose implications are used to adjust the price relative, does not fit the data well (cf. Table 6-13).

In conclusion, if the price relatives are adjusted properly for changing means, they closely follow a random walk and hence are serially uncorrelated. The only exceptions occur when the adjustment procedure is known to be faulty (because the term structure hypothesis used for estimating the expected price relative is invalid). There seems little doubt that price sequences at these maturities would also closely approximate a random walk if the correct term structure hypothesis for *these* maturities could be discovered and used for measuring the expected price change.

NOTES

1. $r_{n,t}$ is the one-period forward rate observed in period t which applies to period $t + n - 1$.

2. $R_{n,t}$ is the n-period spot yield observed in period t. Here, the subscripts will be measured in units of weeks.

3. This suggests a definition for a "thin" market. A market is thin, not when few people participate, but when little new information becomes available each period. The causative direction is from thinness to number of traders, not the other way around. Much new information would attract many traders.

4. When $\alpha = 2$ (the Gaussian distribution), s^2 is one-half the variance. When $\alpha = 1$ (the Cauchy distribution), s is the semi-interquartile range.

5. We shall not measure the skewness parameter but shall simply check how skewed the empirical distributions seem to be.

6. A standardized stable distribution has a location parameter of zero and a scale parameter of unity.

7. For $1 \leqslant \alpha \leqslant 2$, $x_{.72} - x_{.28}$ ranges from 1.648 to 1.66.

8. This fact was first noted by E. Fama.

9. It may seem strange to talk of bias here because the first moment of the ratio of two normally distributed variables does not exist since the variable in the denominator has a finite density at zero. The denominator here, however, is only asymptotically normal and its range extends only over positive, nonzero real numbers.

10. The author has tried plotting the standardized (by $\hat{s}$) empirical distributions on normal probability paper and comparing these by eye with plots of known stable distributions. This method is faulty, however, since the observer tends to place undue emphasis on observations in the extreme tails, these being the most striking on normal probability graphs, *and* the extreme observations have the greatest sampling variance (this variance being inversely proportional to the height of the density function, which is, of course, smallest in the extreme tails).

Another method that has the virtue of providing joint estimates of s and α, and which the author thinks is by far the most promising, is due to Kleinman (1965). Kleinman's method is to estimate the parameters from the sample characteristic function. Unfortunately, the author has thus far been unable to implement his approach.

11. In repeated samples of size 299 from a symmetric stable distribution with $\alpha = 1.20$, the random variable is really not α but $\hat{x}_{.95}$, which will fall between 4.1 and 4.9 about half the time. Since the curves are parallel over short segments, however, this vertical confidence interval can be converted

by a projection on the "mean . . ." curve and used horizontally as a confidence interval on α based on the value of $\hat{x}_{.95}$ actually obtained from the data, in this case 4.48.

12. The values of these means are reported later in Tables 6-10, 6-13, and 6-16.

13. The number of degrees of freedom is equal to the number of classes minus one, minus one for each of the three parameters estimated from the data, i.e., $22 - 1 - 3 = 18$.

Since the statistic above is only asymptotically distributed as χ^2, the deviation of the actual distribution from χ^2 was checked by a simulation on known symmetric stable ($\alpha = 1.3$) data. A total of 101 replications of random samples of 299 each was performed and the results are given below:

Statistic	Simulation	Expected Value
Mean	18.9	18.0
Median	17.5	17.3
Standard deviation	6.39	6.0
Fractiles		
.25	14.5	13.7
.75	22.3	21.6
.90	27.1	26.0
.99	33.9	34.8

The fit seems fairly good for sample sizes this large or larger.

14. If $E(\widetilde{X}_{t-1})$ and $E(\widetilde{X}_t)$ exist, a sufficient condition for the existence of the covariance, i.e., the convergence of the covariance integral, is that $E(\widetilde{X}_t \mid X_{t-1})$ is a bounded function of X_{t-1}. This is obvious from (6-5). Note that the covariance may often exist even if the second and higher moments of X_{t-1} do not. In particular, if $E(\widetilde{X}_{t-1})$ and $E(\widetilde{X}_t)$ exist and if the underlying sequence in Y is a martingale, the covariance is always finite and equal to zero.

15. See equation (6-3).

16. Under certain assumptions, however, linear independence implies complete independence. For instance, if X_t and X_{t-1} have a joint normal distribution and are uncorrelated, they are independent. This may be true for any symmetric bivariate distribution.

17. This is true of the sample covariance if and only if the population covariance is zero.

18. The development in this section is analogous to that usually performed for regression analysis in econometrics; viz., the distribution of the regression coefficients are given *conditional on the observed set of independent variables*. Then, the conditional inferences about the coefficients are shown to hold unconditionally provided that the distribution of the independent variables does not involve the parameters of the model (the true coefficients and the scale parameter of the distribution of the disturbance term).

19. We use .5 truncated sample means for these estimates.

20. *Proof:*

1. The bias in the sample covariance is easily proved to be

$$\text{cov}(\widetilde{U}, \widetilde{V}) - E(\widetilde{C}_{U_t V_t}) = (1/N) \, \text{cov}(\widetilde{U}, \widetilde{V})$$

See, e.g., Kendall and Stuart (1963, p. 308, first equation under 13.2). Hence, when cov $(\widetilde{U}, \widetilde{V}) = 0$, the sample covariance is unbiased.

2. The symmetry of the sample conditional covariance $(C_{U_t V_t} \mid \mathbf{U})$ is proved as follows: The characteristic function of each dependent observation $v_t = V_t - \overline{V}$ is

$$\varphi(\tau) = \exp(-\gamma \, | \tau \, |^{\alpha})$$

where $\gamma = s^{\alpha}$ is the scale parameter, α is the characteristic exponent, and τ is an argument.

The characteristic function of the conditional sample covariance is thus

$$\varphi[C_{U_t V_t} \mid \mathbf{U}, \tau] = \exp\left(-\gamma \sum_{t=1}^{N} \mid \frac{u_t}{N} \tau \mid^{\alpha}\right)$$

and symmetry is shown by the absence of an imaginary part (Lukacs, 1960, pp. 97-107).

We know of no way to prove symmetry of the *unconditional* sample covariance when the underlying distributions are nonnormal stable and the population covariance is zero. In the normal case, however, k-statistic formulas can be used. See, e.g., Kendall and Stuart (1963, p. 322, equation 13.61). It is likely that the similar but unknown formulas hold for the nonnormal cases.

21. This test admits no measure of a type II error since its validity is dependent on the truth of the null hypothesis that the population covariance is zero.

22. Recall that these are conditional expectations and that the equation is more formally expressed as $E_{t-1}(\widetilde{r}_{j,t} \mid B_{t-1}) = r_{j+1,t-1}$, where B_{t-1} is the information state as of $t - 1$.

23. Note that the covariance does *not* involve lagged variables. Its form is cov(Y_t, X_t), where $Y_t = r_{j,t} - r_{j+1,t-1}$ and $X_t = r_{j+1,t-1} - r_{j+2,t-2}$. Thus, $X_t \neq Y_{t-1}$ because $Y_{t-1} = r_{j,t-1} - r_{j+1,t-1} \neq r_{j+1,t-1} - r_{j+2,t-2}$.

24. This standard statistical technique is discussed in many texts. See, e.g., Cramer (1946, pp. 441 and 442).

25. Notational reminder: C is the sample covariance, an estimate of the population covariance. $\hat{s}(C)$ is an estimate of the *scale parameter* of the sample covariance [given by (6-10)].

26. The extra two periods in the $31 + 2$ term are necessary to prevent overlapping since the covariances contain terms that are lagged by two calendar weeks.

27. This section has no bearing on the remaining analysis and can be omitted by those with no particular interest in liquidity premiums.

28. Note, from Table 6-9, that since Aj is a constant, $R_{j,t} - R_{j+1,t-1}$ is serially uncorrelated under this hypothesis.

29. This is not evidence against the hypothesis, however, because $E_{t-1}(\widetilde{R}_{j,t} - R_{j+1,t-1}) = A_j$, and A_j can be nonzero.

30. That is, the .5 truncated sample mean.

31. None of the other six sample means was significantly nonzero when holiday-associated observations were dropped from the sample. See pp. 47-49 for a discussion of holidays.

32. To see that (6-12) actually involves a liquidity premium, recall that

$$R_{j+1,t-1} = \sum_{k=1}^{j+1} \frac{r_{k,t-1}}{j+1} = \frac{1}{j+1} \left\{ \sum_{k=2}^{j+1} [E_{t-1}(\widetilde{R}_{1,t+k-2}) + L_{k,t-1}] + R_{1,t-1} \right\}$$

Thus $R_{j+1,t-1}$ embodies the current one-period rate plus an average of expected future one-period rates and liquidity premiums.

Chapter 7

Summary

This study was separated into a theoretical segment, Chapters 1 through 4, and an empirical segment, Chapters 5 and 6. Although they are linked, it is convenient to summarize the results of each separately.

THEORETICAL RESULTS

Capital Asset Pricing

Chapter 1 suggested that models of security price behavior will not generally be successful in describing data unless they take account of changing *expected returns* over time. The role of capital asset pricing theory is to provide measures of these expected returns.

This suggestion was strongly supported by the empirical examination of Treasury bill price behavior in Chapter 6, where it was shown that bill log price relatives are highly serially dependent but that the dependence is primarily due to changes over time in expected returns.

Efficient Market Model

Chapter 2 was an explicit statement of the efficient market model of security price behavior. The model is a generalization of the famous random walk model and shares the latter's implication that mechanical trading rules will not work.

Instead of a random walk, however, the efficient market model implies that security prices follow submartingale sequences and that the present values of market prices, discounted by appropriate expected returns, follow pure martingale sequences.

Equilibrium Term Structure

Given a few general assumptions about investor behavior, Chapter 3 derived a static equilibrium term structure (i.e., a set of equilibrium forward rates). This derivation discussed how the output of market action depends on the inputs, that is, how equilibrium forward rates depend on investor utility functions (and risk and maturity preferences), investor expectations of future spot yields, investor resources, and states of investor information.

The commonly used liquidity premium, defined as the difference between the forward rate and a corresponding expected future spot yield, was shown to be a complex function of all the investor characteristics mentioned above. The liquidity premium for *each* maturity was shown to depend not only on the distribution of these characteristics across *investors* but also on the pattern of each investors' characteristics across *maturities*. This result should give pause to those (including the author) who would postulate some simple dynamic behavior for liquidity premiums.

Fundamental Dynamic Interest Rate Equation

In addition to deriving a static equilibrium term structure model, Chapter 3 utilized the work of Samuelson (1965) in deriving the fundamental dynamic interest rate equation for an efficient market. This equation states that the forward rate, minus the liquidity premium, follows a pure martingale sequence.

Term Structure Theories

Using the fundamental dynamic interest rate equation, Chapter 4 showed how the various term structure hypotheses could be used to derive *testable* equations. The basic method was to form models of liquidity premium behavior and substitute them in the fundamental equation. The liquidity premium model for the time-dependent market segmentation hypothesis was original here, but the others were given or suggested in past research.

Three sets of equations were developed. Each set, depending on one term structure hypothesis, includes dynamic behavioral equations for forward rates, yields, and prices. They are summarized in Table 6-9.

EMPIRICAL RESULTS

A minor contribution of the present research was collection of a large body of data on U.S. Treasury bill rates. These data, reported on in Chapter 5, should prove to be of further value to those interested in the Treasury bill market. (A copy of the data is available from the author, of course.)

The primary empirical results of the study were obtained in Chapter 6 by application of new statistical methods to the data analysis.

Statistical Methods

Chapter 6 contains the first attempt to apply recent developments in the mathematical theory of stable distributions. A procedure suggested by Fama and Roll (1968) was used to estimate the scale parameters of the empirical distributions of interest rate changes. A method *implied* by their work was used to estimate the distributions' characteristic exponents. In accordance with their monte carlo results, the .5 truncated mean was utilized as a measure of scale, and the asymptotic standard error of the .5 truncated mean was tabulated here for the first time.

After the distribution parameters were estimated, Chapter 6 presented methods for testing stable variates for martingale behavior. A scale parameter was derived for the sample covariance by utilizing stable distribution theory and the work of Wise (1963).

Empirical Tests

These new statistical methods were used to test three equations implied by hypotheses of the term structure. The pure expectations hypothesis performed poorly and was rejected by most of the tests. The other hypotheses, the time-dependent market segmentation hypothesis and the liquidity preference-stationary market segmentation hypothesis, performed well.

Price behavior of government bills was also examined. The log price relative was found to be highly serially dependent. However, when the changing expected return was accounted for by using the implications of a successfully tested term structure hypothesis, the adjusted log price relative was serially independent for most maturities. This indicates that the government bill market conforms closely to the efficient market model.

Appendix
Qualifications and Adjuncts

QUALIFICATIONS

There are probably a very large number of different hedges one could use to qualify the results but we shall mention only four: (1) alternative forms for the relationship between expected returns and liquidity premiums, (2) alternative models of the term structure hypotheses, (3) correlation in empirical results across maturities, and (4) errors in the data.

1. On page 21, an additive form was given for the "typical" relationship among forward rates, liquidity premiums, and expected future spot rates. This additive form was selected because it is generally implied in the literature of the term structure. Instead, however, of having

$$_j r_{k,t}^i = {}_j L_{k,t}^i + E_t^i (R_{1,t+k-1} \mid B_t^i)$$

we could just as well have used a multiplicative form such as

$$_j r_{k,t}^i = ({}_j L_{k,t}^i) [E_t^i (R_{1,t+k-1} \mid B_t^i)]$$

Indeed, some proponents of the liquidity preference hypothesis seem to suggest a relationship like this when they argue that the effect of liquidity premiums is a function of the level of interest rates. See, e.g., Kessel (1965, p. 25).

If a multiplicative form had been used here, all the testable equations would have been different. We can hope that the empirical conclusions about the "best" term structure hypotheses and the efficiency of the bill market would have remained the same, but, of course, we are not guaranteed that this would have been the case.

2. The two models of liquidity premium behavior, equations (4-6) and (4-10), are reasonable but somewhat arbitrary. More complicated models could be postulated and some of them might perform better in the empirical tests. However, the simple models (4-6) and (4-10) do surprisingly (?) well empirically and the principle of Occam's razor[1] can be invoked in their support.

3. In Chapter 6, the reader may have obtained the impression that the empirical results are independent across maturities. Quite the opposite is true. The results are highly correlated among maturities, and as a consequence Chapter 6 does not contain 24 to 26 independent tests of each hypothesis (i.e., an independent test at each maturity).

Evidence that the entire yield curve moves synchronously is available from many sources. For instance, Tables 6-14 and 6-17 indicate this fact. Note that the signs of the covariances in these tables cluster in subperiods, tending to be mostly positive or mostly negative in any given subperiod and rarely being about equal in number. In Table 6-14, part 2, for example, 8 of the 16 subperiods have 20 or more plus signs and 5 subperiods have 5 or less plus signs out of a possible 24. This leaves only 3 subperiods with a number of plus signs between 5 and 20.

Synchronous movements of yields are also evidenced by Meiselman's "error-learning model" test results.[2]

In addition, Table A-1 provides further evidence with correlation coefficients between the one-period yield, forward rates, and yields for longer maturities (for the bill data used here). Since all longer-term rates are correlated with the one-period rate, they are obviously correlated with each other.

4. Despite many precautions, it *is* possible that the data contain errors. The yield quotations given on the dealers' published cards may not always be firm. The quotations are daily closing *bids* and *askeds*. Although unlikely, no transactions need ever have been made at these prices. This may be particularly true of the quotations at the new issue maturities, 13 and 26 weeks.

TABLE A-1   Correlation Coefficients Between the One-Week Yield and Longer-Term Yields and Forward Rates, U.S. Treasury Bills, 1949-1964[a]

Maturity, n (weeks)	ρ $(R_{n,t}, R_{1,t})$	ρ $(R_{1,t}, r_{n,t})$	Maturity, n (weeks)	ρ $(R_{1,t}, R_{n,t})$	ρ $(R_{1,t}, r_{n,t})$
2	.994	.977	13	.947	.822
3	.990	.956	14	.878	.637
4	.985	.928	15	.879	.612
5	.979	.891	16	.874	.575
6	.974	.873	17	.868	.525
7	.970	.866	18	.860	.518
8	.966	.858	19	.848	.400
9	.962	.838	20	.838	.412
10	.959	.841	21	.829	.362
11	.955	.860	22	.818	.347
12	.955	.864	23	.807	.335
			24	.799	.387
			25	.787	.343

[a]Sample sizes: maturities 2-12, 796; maturity 13, 768; maturities 14-25, 305.

Errors in the variables introduce negative biases in the covariance tests of serial correlation (and into the χ^2 tests of serial dependence). This is because the typical covariance is

$$\text{cov}(R_t - R_{t-1}, R_{t-1} - R_{t-2})$$

where R_{t-1} appears in both variables with opposite signs.

The covariances for the *pure expectations hypothesis* are mainly negative (see Table 6-10). Proponents of this hypothesis might use the possible presence of errors as a basis for criticizing the conclusion that the hypothesis fits poorly. I do not think this argument is justified for two reasons. First, excluding holiday-associated observations, which are known to contain errors, does not appear to change the results substantially. (In 21 out of 35 cases, the sample covariance increased algebraically when holiday-associated observations were excluded.) Second, the means test, which is not biased by errors, rejects the pure expectations hypothesis strongly.

In conclusion, these four qualifications are expressed so that the reader will know they have been considered.[3] None of them seriously restrict the conclusions but they do suggest alternative explanations and alternative lines of attack for replicative endeavors.

POSSIBLE ADJUNCTS

Suggestions for further research are of two types, those that could be attached as appendages to the present document and those that would require a major effort of dissertation proportions. Of the former variety, we mention:

1. The use of dynamic interest rate equations and empirical test procedures contained here for examination of interest rates and prices of securities other than Treasury bills.
2. A study of bill market operations with emphasis on
   a. Precise causes of the peculiar interest rate behavior around new-issue maturities.
   b. Motives for investor bill holdings—Are bills usually held as a hedge against short-term liabilities or as a money substitute or as part of a portfolio.
3. Development of a securities market model which does not use price as the relevant decision variable but instead uses *utility* of present and expected future consumption, averaged across market participants.
4. Development and testing of more complex term structure models, such as, for example, a model of the liquidity preference hypothesis in which the liquidity premium changes in size with the level of interest rates.
5. Use of refined techniques for estimating the parameters of stable distributions (cf. p. 117, footnote 10) and application of these techniques to the distributions of interest rate changes.
6. Examination of interest rate sequences with spectral methods. [In this regard cf. Sargent (1968)].

Research of a more difficult nature is dominated by a single topic: the search for a general, multiperiod, *realistic* (in the sense of fitting data) model of individual consumption and investment that can be summed over individuals to provide a macromodel that explains the market prices of capital assets.

NOTES

1. "Pluralites non est ponenda sine necessitate," William of Ockham (or Occam), c. 1280-1349.

2. Meiselman recognizes that the error-learning model's results could be explained simply by the joint movement of all yields, but he argues that "An empirical regularity is not a theory, and . . . there are [sic] an infinite number of hypotheses consistent with this . . . relationship" (1962, pp. 35-36).

3. They may have been more than just considered. Much time was spent on them, particularly on the errors-in-variables problem, without obtaining any worthwhile, helpful, or contradictory results.

References

Bierwag, G. O., and Grove, M. A. "A Model of the Term Structure of Interest Rates." *The Review of Economics and Statistics*, vol. 49, February 1967.

Cramer, Harald. *Mathematical Methods of Statistics*. Princeton, N.J.: Princeton University Press, 1946.

Fama, Eugene F. "The Behavior of Stock-Market Prices." *Journal of Business*, vol. 38, January 1965.

Fama, Eugene F., and Roll, Richard. "Some Properties of Symmetric Stable Distributions." *Journal of the American Statistical Association*, vol. 63, September 1968.

Feller, William. *An Introduction to Probability Theory and Its Applications*. Vol. II. New York: John Wiley & Sons, Inc., 1966.

Friedman, Milton, and Schwartz, Anna Jacobson. *A Monetary History of the United States, 1867-1960*. A Study by the National Bureau of Economic Research, New York. Princeton: Princeton University Press, 1963.

Hicks, J. R. *Value and Capital*. Oxford: The Clarendon Press, 1946.

Kendall, Maurice G., and Stuart, Alan. *The Advanced Theory of Statistics*. Vol. I. New York: Hafner Publishing Company, 1963.

Kessel, Rueben A. *The Cyclical Behavior of the Term Structure of Interest Rates*. National Bureau of Economic Research Occasional Paper No. 91. New York: Columbia University Press, 1965.

Kleinman, David C. "Estimating the Parameters of Stable Probability Laws." University of Chicago, Graduate School of Business,

Proposed Research Project for the Degree of Doctor of Philosophy, June 1965.

Lukacs, Eugene. *Characteristic Functions.* London: Charles Griffin & Company Limited, 1960.

Lutz, Friedrich A. "The Structure of Interest Rates." *Quarterly Journal of Economics*, vol. 55, 1940-41.

Mandelbrot, Benoit. "Forecasts of Future Prices, Unbiased Markets, and 'Martingale' Models." *Journal of Business*, vol. 39, January 1966.

Marsaglia, George. "Ratios of Normal Variables and Ratios of Sums of Uniform Variables." *Journal of the American Statistical Association*, vol. 60, March 1965.

Meiselman, David. *The Term Structure of Interest Rates.* The Ford Foundation Doctoral Dissertation Series. Englewood Cliffs, N.J.: Prentice-Hall, Inc., 1962.

Miller, Merton H., and Modigliani, Franco. "Dividend Policy, Growth, and the Valuation of Shares." *Journal of Business*, vol. 34, October 1961.

Roll, Richard. "The Efficient Market Model Applied to U.S. Treasury Bill Rates." Unpublished Ph.D. dissertation, The University of Chicago, March 1968.

Samuelson, Paul A. "Proof that Properly Anticipated Prices Fluctuate Randomly." *Industrial Management Review*, vol. 6, Spring 1965.

Sargent, Thomas J. "Interest Rates in the Nineteen-Fifties." *Review of Economics and Statistics*, vol. 50, May 1968.

U.S. Congress, Joint Economic Committee, *A Study of the Dealer Market for Federal Government Securities.* 86th Cong., 2d Sess., 1960.

Wise, John. "Linear Estimators for Linear Regression Systems Having Infinite Residual Variances." Berkeley-Stanford Mathematical Economics Seminar, October 1963.

Index

absorption, by market of new issues, 54, 58-59

acceptance interval, 96-97

accord, between Treasury and Federal Reserve, 52

addition rules for sums of random variables, 86-88

banker's discount, 47; and conversion to true return, 47

basis point, 79

bias, 66, 68, 83, 86; in ratios of normal variates, 117; in sample covariance, 118-119

Bierwag, G. O., 29

binomial distribution, 97

bonds: in an efficient market, 15; market for, 15; noncoupon, 15-17

capital asset pricing, 121, 130

capital gains, accruing to forward loans, 23

Cauchy distribution, 65, 117; sample means from, 87; truncated means from, 85

central limit theorem, generalized, 63, 81

characteristic exponent: estimated for bill yield changes, 69-73; estimator for, 65-68; stable distribution, 64, 91, 124

characteristic function, 119

commodities, perishable and indestructible, 13

competitive equilibrium, 6; dynamic, 15, 32-33, 35; static, 15, 18, 26-32, 122

confidence intervals for stable distributions, 93

consistent estimator, 66

consumption, saving plans and, 24

contingency table tests of serial dependence, 91, 93, 113, 115

convolutions, 86

correlation coefficients between one week yield and longer-term yields, 128

covariance: asymptotic, of adjacent fractiles, 84; definition, 82; distribution of sample, 86-88; existence, 118; proof of zero for martingales, 82-83; sample, 86, 91, 99, 100, 106-108, 118, scale parameter of sample, 86-87, 106; symmetry of sampling distribution, 119

Cramer, H., 65, 119

data validity checks, 50-52

dealers in Treasury bills, 46-47, 54-61; and collusion hypothesis, 58-59; costs of, 59; inventories of, 59; quotation errors by, 128

degrees of freedom: in chi-square test of goodness-of-fit, 76, 118; in contingency table tests, 113

demand: for bonds, 26; cross-elasticities of forward loan, 28; for forward loans, 20

Devine, C. J. & Company, 51

discounted present value of future price, 10

135